AF522097

TEXTBOOK OF WATER CHEMISTRY

By
Dr. Syed Aftab Iqbal
M.Sc. , Ph.D., FICS
FICC, FIAEM, MNASc.
Professor
Department of Chemistry
Saifia Science College
Barkatullah University
Bhopal (India)
&
Dr. Fethi Kooli
Assistant Professor
Department of Chemistry
Taibah University
Madinah Al-Munnawarah (K.S.A.)

DISCOVERY PUBLISHING HOUSE PVT. LTD.
NEW DELHI-110 002

Published by:
Tilak Wasan

DISCOVERY PUBLISHING HOUSE PVT. LTD.
4383/4B, Ansari Road, Darya Ganj
New Delhi-110 002 (India)
Phone : +91-11-23279245, 43596064-65
Fax : +91-11-23253475
E-mail : discoverypublishinghouse@gmail.com
namitwasan9@gmail.com
sales@discoverypublishinggroup.com
web : www.discoverypublishinggroup.com

***First Edition:* 2011**

***Reprinted:* 2018**

ISBN: 978-81-8356-852-4

Textbook of Water Chemistry

Printed at:
Infinity Imaging Systems
Delhi

Preface

Water is a very important substance, as it makes up the larger part of an organism's body. But what exactly is water? Inside the body of a human being there is a skeleton, which makes your body solid and makes sure you can stand up without falling apart. Water is also a kind of skeleton. It consists of tiny particles, the atoms, just like every other substance on earth. One of these atoms is called hydrogen and the other is called oxygen. As you probably know the air that we breathe also contains oxygen. One particle of water is called a molecule. When lots of water molecules melt together we can see the water and drink it or use it, for instance to flush a toilet.

Polarity determines if a substance is water-soluble. A polair substance is a substance that has two kinds of 'poles', as in a magnet. When another substance is also polair the poles of the substances attract each other and as a result the substances mix. A substance then dissolves in water.

Substances that contain no 'poles' are called apolair substances. Oil for instance is an apolair substance, which is why oil does not dissolve in water. In fact it floats on water, just like ice, due to its smaller density.

When water is referred to as 'hard' this simply means, that it contains more minerals than ordinary water. These are especially the minerals calcium and magnesium. The degree of hardness of the water exceeds, when more calcium and magnesium dissolve.

Magnesium and calcium are positively charged ions. Because of their presence, other positively charged substances will dissolve less easy in hard water than in water that does not contain calcium and magnesium. This is the cause of the fact that soap doesn't really dissolve in hard water.

Physical properties of a substance are properties that have everything to do with the substance's appearance. Chemical properties are properties that are often used in chemistry, to address the state of a substance. Physical and chemical properties can tell us something about the behaviour of a substance in certain circumstances.

Author

Contents

1 Introduction

Water is a very important substance, as it makes up the larger part of an organism's body. But what exactly is water? Inside the body of a human being there is a skeleton, which makes your body solid and makes sure you can stand up without falling apart. Water is also a kind of skeleton. It consists of tiny particles, the atoms, just like every other substance on earth. One of these atoms is called hydrogen and the other is called oxygen. As you probably know the air that we breathe also contains oxygen. One particle of water is called a molecule. When lots of water molecules melt together we can see the water and drink it or use it, for instance to flush a toilet.

How is a water molecule built up?

A water molecule consists of three atoms; an oxygen atom and two hydrogen atoms, which are bond together like little magnets. The atoms consist of matter that has a nucleus in the centre.

The difference between atoms is expressed by atomic numbers. The atomic number of an atom depends on the number of protons in the nucleus of the atom. Protons are small positively charged particles. Hydrogen has one proton in the nucleus and oxygen has eight. There are also uncharged particles in the nucleus, called neutrons.

Next to protons and neutrons, atoms also consist of negatively charged electrons, which can be found in the electron cloud around the nucleus. The number of electrons in an atom equals the number of protons in the nucleus. The attraction between the protons and electrons is what keeps an atom together.

How much does a water molecule weigh?

The weight of a molecule is determined by the atomic masses of the atoms that it is built of. The atomic mass of an atom is determined by the addition of the number of protons and neutrons in the nucleus, because the electrons hardly weigh anything. When the atomic masses of the separate atoms are known, one simply has to add them up to find the total atomic mass of a molecule, expressed in grams per mol. A mol is an expression of the molair weight of a molecule, derived from the weight of a hydrogen molecule, which is 1 mol. Hydrogen has a relative atomic mass of 1 g/mol and oxygen has a relative atomic mass of 16 g/mol. Water consists of one oxygen atom and two hydrogen atoms. This means that the mass of a water molecule is 1g + 1g + 16g = 18 g/ mol.

When the number of moles of water is known, one can calculate how many grams of weight this is, by using the molar weight of water. The molair weight of separate atoms can be found in the periodic table of Mendelejef. In what states (phases) can water be found?

Water exists in three states: solid, liquid and gaseous. At a normal temperature of about 25 °C it is liquid, but below 0 °C it will freeze and turn to ice. Water can be found in the gaseous state above 100 °C, this is called the boiling point of water, at which water starts to evaporate. The water turns to gas and is then odourless and colourless. How fast water evaporates depends on the temperature; if the temperature is high, water will evaporate sooner.

What happens if water changes phase?

The changes from a liquid to a solid or to a gas are called phase changes. When a substance such as water changes phase, its physical appearance changes, but not its chemical properties. This is because the chemical structure remains the same, but the molecules of which it consists will float a little further apart. In the solid state the water molecules are fairly close together, but in the liquid state they are a bit further apart. The water becomes liquid as a result of parting molecules. When water changes from liquid to gas the molecules will part even further, that is why we cannot detect it.

Why does ice float on water?

When substances freeze, usually the molecules come closer together. Water has an abnormality there: it freezes below 0 °C, but when temperatures goes below 4 °C, water starts to expand again and as a result the density becomes lower. Density of a substance means the weight in kilograms of a cubic metre of a substance. When two substances are mixed but do not dissolve in one another, the substance with the lowest density floats on the other substance. In this case that substance is ice, due to the decreased density of water.

How come not all substances are water-soluble?

Polarity determines if a substance is water-soluble. A polair substance is a substance that has two kinds of 'poles', as in a magnet. When another substance is also polair the poles of the substances attract each other and as a result the substances mix. A substance then dissolves in water.

Substances that contain no 'poles' are called apolair substances. Oil for instance is an apolair substance, which is why oil does not dissolve in water. In fact it floats on water, just like ice, due to its smaller density.

What is hard water?

When water is referred to as 'hard' this simply means, that it contains more minerals than ordinary water. These are especially the minerals calcium and magnesium. The degree of hardness of the water exceeds, when more calcium and magnesium dissolve.

Magnesium and calcium are positively charged ions. Because of their presence, other positively charged substances will dissolve less easy in hard water than in water that does not contain calcium and magnesium. This is the cause of the fact that soap doesn't really dissolve in hard water.

What are physical and chemical properties?

Physical properties of a substance are properties that have everything to do with the substance's appearance. Chemical properties are properties that are often used in chemistry, to address the state of a substance. Physical and chemical properties can tell us something about the behaviour of a substance in certain circumstances.

Which physical and chemical properties does water have?

There are several different physical and chemical properties, which are often used alternately. We can name the following:

— Density. The density of water means the weight of a certain amount of water. It is usually expressed in kilograms per cubic metre. (physical)

— Thermal properties. This refers to what happens to water when it is heated; at which temperature it becomes gaseous and that sort of thing. (physical)

— Conductivity. This means the amount of electricity that water can conduct. It is expressed in a chemical magnitude. (physical)

— Light absorption. This is the amount of light a certain amount of water can absorb over time. (chemical)

— Viscosity. This means the syrupiness of water and it determines the mobility of water. When the temperature rises, the viscosity degrades; this means that water will be more mobile at higher temperatures. (physical)

— The pH. The pH has its own scale, running up from 1 to 14. The pH shows whether a substance is acid (pH 1-6), neutral (pH 7) or basic (pH 8-14). The number of hydrogen atoms in the substance determines the pH. The more hydrogen atoms a substance contains, the lower the pH will be. A substance that contains many hydrogen atoms is acid. We can measure the pH by dipping a special colouring paper in the substance, the colours shows which pH the substance has. (chemical)

— Alkalinity. This is the capacity of water to neutralize an acid or a base, so that the pH of the water will not change. (chemical)

Water is an unusual compound with unique physical properties. As a result, its the compound of life. Yet, its the most abundant compound in the biosphere of Earth. These properties are related to its electronic structure, bonding, and chemistry. However, due to its affinity for a variety of substances, ordinary water contains other substances. Few of us has used, seen or tested pure water, based on which we discuss its chemistry.

The chemistry of water deals with the fundamental chemical property and information about water. Water chemistry is discussed in the following subtitles:

- Composition of water
- Structure and bonding of water
- Molecular Vibration of water
- Symmetry of water molecules
- Formation of hydrogen bonding in water
- Structure of ice
- Autoionization
- Leveling effect of water and acid-base characters
- Amphiprotic nature
- Reactivity of water towards alkali metals; alkaline earth metals; halogens; hydrides; methane; oxides; and oxygen ions.
- Electrolysis of water
- Composition of water.

Water consists of only hydrogen and oxygen. Both elements have natural stable and radioactive isotopes. Due to these isotopes, water molecules of masses roughly 18 ($H_2{}^{16}O$) to 22 ($D_2{}^{18}O$) are expected to form. Isotopes and their abundances of H and O are given below. From these data, we can estimate the relative abundances of all isotopic water molecules.

The predominant water molecules $H_2{}^{16}O$ have a mass of 18 amu, but molecules with mass 19 and 20 occur significantly. Because the isotopic abundances are not always the same due to their astronomical origin. The isotopic distribution of water molecules depends on its source and age. Its study is linked to other sciences. Chemistry of water and water pollution, Ellis Harwood for isotopic distribution of water.

Abundances (% or halflife) of hydrogen and oxygen isotopes					
H	^{2}D	^{3}T			
99.985%	0.015%	12.33 y			
^{14}O	^{15}O	^{16}O	^{17}O	^{18}O	
70.6 s	122 s	99.762%	0.038%	0.200%	
Relative abundance of isotopic water					
$H_2{}^{16}O$	$H_2{}^{18}O$	$H_2{}^{17}O$	$HD^{16}O$	$D_2{}^{16}O$	$HT^{16}O$
99.78%	0.20%	0.03%	0.0149%	0.022 ppm	trace
18	20	19	19	20	20 amu

In particular, $D_2{}^{16}O$ is called heavy water, and it is produced by enrichment from natural water. Properties of heavy water are particularly interesting due to its application in nuclear technology.

Structure and Bonding of the Water Molecule

Pure water, H_2O, has a unique molecular structure. The O-H bondlengths are 0.096 nm and the H-O-H angle = 104.5°. This strange geometry can be explained by various methods.

From carbon to neon, the numbers of valence electrons increase from 4 to 8. These elements require 4, 3, 2, 1, and 0 H atoms to share electrons in order to complete the octet requirement. Their Lewis dot structures are shown on the right, and note the trend in bondlengths.

There are six valance electrons on the oxygen, and one each from the hydrogen atom in the water molecule. The eight electrons form two H-O bonds, and left two lone pairs. The long pairs and bonds stay away from each other and they extend towards the corners of a tetrahedron. Such an ideal structure should give H-O-H bond angle of 109.5°, but the lone pairs repel each other more than they repel the O-H bonds. Thus, the O-H bonds are pushed closer, making the H-O-H angle less than 109°.

After the introduction of quantum mechanics, the electronic configuration for the valence electron of oxygen are 2s2 2p4. Since the energy levels of 2s and 2p are close, valence electrons have characters of both s and p. The mixture is called sp3 hybridization. These hybridized orbitals are shown on the right. The structures of CH_4, NH_3, and H_2O can all explained by these hybrid orbitals of the central atoms. The above approach is the valence bond theory, and both the C-H bonds and lone electron pairs are counted as VSPER pairs in the Valence-shell Electron-Pair Repulsion (VSEPR) model, according to which, the four groups point to the corners of a tetrahedron.

For triatomic molecules such as water, molecular orbital (MO) approach can also be applied to discuss the bonding. The result however is similar to the valence bond approach, but the MO theory gives the energy levels of the electron for further exploration.

Molecular Vibration of Water

Atoms in a molecule are never at rest, and for each type of molecule, there are some normal vibration modes. For the water molecule, the three normal modes of vibrations are symmetric stretching, bending and assymmetric stretching.

The vibrations are quantized, as do any microscopic system, and their quantum numbers are designated as v1, v2 and v3. The observed transition bands of D_2O, H_2O, and HDO are given in the table on the right.

The ideal transition bands are centered in the given wave numbers. However, these wave numbers are calculated based on isolated molecules with no interaction with any neighbour. When molecules interact with each other, the energy levels are modified, and the bands shift.

Many more less intense absorption bands extend into the green part of the visible spectrum. The absorption spectrum of water may contribute to the blue color for lake, river and ocean waters.

Symmetry of Water Molecules

The water molecules are rather symmetric in that there are two mirror planes of symmetry, one containing all three atoms and one perpendicular to the plane passing through the bisector of the H-O-H angle. Furthermore, if the molecules are rotated 180° (360°/2) the shape of the molecule is unperturbed. This indicates that the molecules have a 2-fold rotation axis. The three symmetry elements are 2-fold rotation, and two mirror planes. Both mirror planes contain the rotation axis, and this type of symmetry belongs to the point group C2v.

A point group has a definite number of symmetry elements arranged in certain fashion. Molecules can be classified according to their point groups. Molecules of the same point group have similar spectroscopic characters. Other molecules of C2v point group are CH_2=O, CH_2Cl_2, the bent O_3 etc.

Formation of Hydrogen Honding

Under certain conditions, an atom of hydrogen is attracted by rather strong forces to two atoms instead of only one, so that it may be considered to be acting as a bond between them. This is called hydrogen bond. The Nature of the Chemical Bond. He gave the ion [F:H:F]- as an example. At that time, the hydrogen bond was recognized as mainly ionic in nature. The energy associated with hydrogen bond is 8 to 40 kJ/mol.

Normally, the melting point and boiling point of a substance increase with molecular mass. For example the melting points of inert gases are 0.95, 24.48, 83.8, and 116.6 K respectively for He, Ne, Ar, and Kr.

In this table, the melting and boiling points for water are particular high for its small molecular mass. This is usually attributed to the formation of hydrogen bonds. The small electronegative atoms F, O and N are somewhat negatively charged when they are bonded to hydrogen atoms. The negative charges on F, O and N attract the slightly positive hydrogen atoms, forming a strong interaction called hydrogen bond.

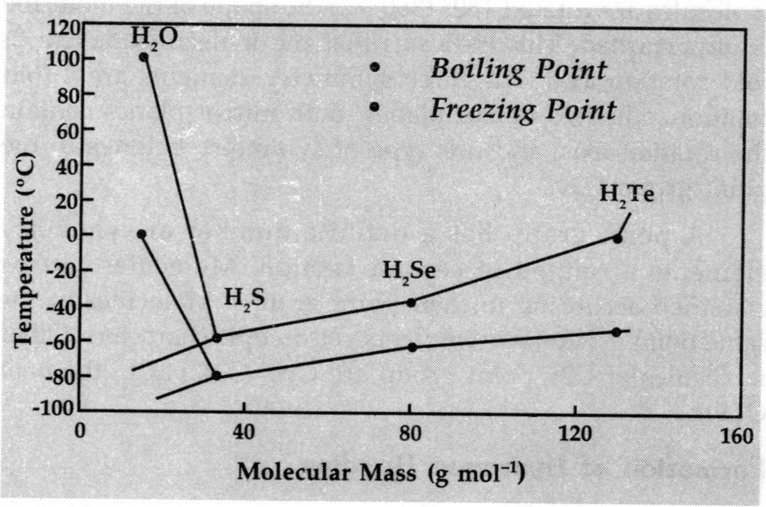

Fig. 1.1

Boiling and Freezing Points of Group 16 Hydrides

Based on the observed absorption at 3546 and 3691 cm^{-1}, Van Thiel, Becker, and Pinmentel suggested the formation of water dimer when trapped in a matrix of nitrogen.

Due to hydrogen bonding, water molecules form dimers, trimers, polymers, and clusters. The hydrogen bonds are not necessarily liner.

Structure of Ice

Ice occurs in many places, including the Antarctic. If all the ice melted, the water level of the oceans will rise about 70 m. The structure of ice and the caption are from this link.

The density of ice is dramatically smaller than that of water, due to the regular arrangement of water molecule via hydrogen bonds. In an idealized structure of ice, every hydrogen atom is involved in hydrogen bond. Every oxygen atom is surrounded by four hydrogen bonds.

The tetrahedral coordination opens up the space between molecules. On each hydrogen bond, shown by a rod joining the oxygen atoms, lies one proton in an asymmetric position (not shown). Bond lengths, 275 pm, are indicated. Ordinary ice is hexagonal and the hexagonal c axis is labelled 732 pm, and one of the hexagonal a axes is labelled 450 pm. If water vapor condenses on very cold substrate at 143-193 K (-130 to -80°C) a cubic phase is formed. In (b) the cubic unit cell is outlined with dashed lines; dimensions are in pm determined at 110 K.

These diagrams can also be used to represent the two forms of diamond, and in this case, the rods joining the atoms represent C-C bonds. Each C-C bondlength is 154 pm. Silicon and germanium crystals have the same structure, but their bondlengths are longer. The two diamond types of structure are related to the packing of spheres. The hexagonal type has the ABABAB ... sequence, whereas the cubic type has the ABCABC ... sequence. In both cases, half of UUsting.

The Autoionization of Water

The Autoionization of Water in the formation of ions according to

$$HOH(l) + HOH(l) = H_3O^+ + OH^-$$

This is an equilibrium process and is characterised by an equilibrium constant, K'_w:

$$K'_w = \frac{\left[H_3O^+\right]\left[OH^-\right]}{\left[H_2O\right]}$$

Since $[H_2O] = 1000/18 = 55.56$ M, and remains rather constant under any circumstance, we usually write:

$$K_w = [H_3O^+]\,[OH^-]$$
$$= 10^{-14} \text{ (or 1e-14)}$$
$$pK_w = -\log K_w \text{ (defined)}$$
$$= 14 \text{ (at 298 K)}$$

For neutral water, $[H_3O^+] = [OH^-] = 1e\text{-}7$ at this temperature. Furthermore, we define:

$$pH = -\log[H_3O^+]$$
$$pOH = -\log[OH^-]$$
$$pH = pOH = 7 \text{ at 298 K; (in neutral solutions)}$$

Levelling Effect of Water and Acid-base Characters

The strength of strong acids and bases is dominated by the autoionization of water. In aqueous solutions, the strongest acid and base are the hydronium ion, H_3O^+, and the hydroxide ion OH^- respectively. Acids HCl, HBr, HI, HNO_3, $HClO_3$, $HClO_4$, and H_2SO_4 completely ionize in water, making them as strong as H_3O^+ due to the leveling effect of water. Furthermore, strong acids, strong bases, and salts completely ionize in their aqueous solutions.

For example, HCl is a stronger acid than H_2O, and the reaction takes place as HCl dissolves in water.

$$HCl + H_2O = Cl^- + H_3O^+$$

A similar equation can be written for another strong acid.

On the other hand, a strong base also react with water to give the strong base species, OH^-.

$$H_2O + B^- = OH^- + HB$$

For example, O_2^-, CH_3O^-, and NH_3 are strong bases. The leveling effect also apply to bases.

Amphiprotic Species

Equilibria of acids and bases, are interesting chemistry. When an acid and a base differ by a proton, they are called a conjugate acid-base pair. A water molecule is a weak acid and base, due to its ability to accept or donate a proton. Such properties make water an amphiprotic species. In fact, H_3O^+, H_2O and OH^- are amphiprotic, as are some other conjugate acid-base pairs of weak acids and bases.

If several acids and bases are dissolved in water, all equilibria must be considered. To estimate the pH of these solutions requires the exact treatment of several equilibrium constants. For example, many species dissolve in rain water, and many equilibria must be considered. Detail consideration and examples are given in Acid-Base Reactions.

Discussion

Generally speaking, rain water has a pH about 5, rather acidic. It dissolves limestone and marble readily. Due to the dissolved carbon dioxide, rain water is a buffer solution.

Increased carbon dioxide level forces an increase in dissolved carbon dioxide. Would this causes pH of rain water to decrease or increase? Justify your answer by giving the reasons.

Since $[H^+] = 2.0e\text{-}5$, $[OH^-] = 5e\text{-}9$, the amount of H^+ from ionization of water is also 5.0e-9, small with respect to 2.0e-5 from ionization of H_2CO_3. Similarly, the ionization from

$$HCO_3^- \rightleftharpoons CO_3^{2-} + H^+$$

is also small. Most of the C-containing species is H_2CO_3

H_2CO_3 is a weak acid, its ionization is small indeed.

Now, you may proceed to evaluate other concentrations:

$[OH^-]$, $[HCO_3^-]$, and $[CO_3^{2-}]$

Reactivity of Water Towards Metals

Alkali metals react with water readily. Contact of cesium metal with water causes immediate explosion, and the reactions become slower for potassium, sodium and lithium. Reaction with barium, strontium, calcium are less well known, but they do react readily. Warm water may be needed to react with calcium metal, however.

Many metals displace H^+ ions in acidic solutions. This is often seen as a property of acids.

Electrolysis of Water

The enthalpy of formation for liquid water, $H_2O(l)$, is -285.830 and that of water vapour is -241.826 kJ/mol. The difference is the heat of vaporization at 298 K. Liquid water and vapor entropies (S) are 69.95 and 188.835 kJ K^{-1} mol^{-1} respectively. These are entropies, not standard entropies of formation. The entropy of formation for water is obtained by:

DSof water = Sowater - SoH_2 - 0.5 SoO_2 = 69.95 - 130.68 - 0.5*205.14 (data from Thermodynamic Data) = - 163.3 J K-1 mol-1

DGowater = DH - T DS (note H in kJ/mol and S in J/mol)

DGowater = -285.83 - 298.15 * 163.3/1000 = -237.13 kJ

The equilibrium constant and Gibb's energy are related:

DGo = - R T ln K

K = exp(- DGo / R T) = 3.5e41 atm-3/2

This is a very large value for the formation of water,

$H_2 + 0.5\ O_2 = 0.5\ H_2O(l)$.

In other words, the reaction is complete, and the possibility of water dissociated into hydrogen and oxygen is very small. A negative value for DGo indicates an exothermic reaction.

The Gibb's energy is the energy released other than pressure-volume work. This redox reaction to form water can be engineered to proceed in a Daniel cell. In this case, the energy is converted into electric energy according to this equation.

DGo water = - n F E = -237.13 kJ

where n is the number of electrons (= 2) in the redox equation, F is the Faraday constant (= 96485 C), and E is the potential of the Daniel cell. Thus,

$$E = -\frac{-237130J}{2 * 96485C} = 1.23\ V$$

Ideally, a reverse voltage of 1.23 V is required for the electrolysis of water. But in reality, a little over voltage is required to carry out the electrolysis to decompose water. Furthermore, pure water does not conduct electricity, and acid, base or salt is often added for the electrolysis of water. This link has a demonstration.

2 Water

Water is a common chemical substance that is essential for the survival of all known forms of life. In typical usage, water refers only to its liquid form or state, but the substance also has a solid state, ice, and a gaseous state, water vapor or steam. Water covers 71% of the Earth's surface. On Earth, it is found mostly in oceans and other large water bodies, with 1.6% of water below ground in aquifers and 0.001% in the air as vapor, clouds (formed of solid and liquid water particles suspended in air), and precipitation. Saltwater oceans hold 97% of surface water, glaciers and polar ice caps 2.4%, and other land surface water such as rivers, lakes and ponds 0.6%. A very small amount of the Earth's water is contained within biological bodies and manufactured products. Other water is trapped in ice caps, glaciers, aquifers, or in lakes, sometimes providing fresh water for life on land.

Water moves continually through a cycle of evaporation or transpiration (evapotranspiration), precipitation, and runoff, usually reaching the sea. Winds carry water vapour over land at the same rate as runoff into the sea, about 36 Tt (1012 kilograms) per year. Over land, evaporation and transpiration contribute another 71 Tt per year to the precipitation of 107 Tt per year over land. Clean, fresh drinking water is essential to human and other life. Access to safe drinking water has improved steadily over the past decades in almost every part of the world. However, some observers have estimated that by 2025 more than half of the world population will be facing water-based vulnerability, a situation which has been called a water crisis by the United Nations. Water plays an important role in the world economy, as it functions as a solvent for a wide variety of chemical substances and facilitates industrial cooling and transportation. Approximately 70 per cent of freshwater is consumed by agriculture.

Types of Water

Water can appear in three states; it is one of the very few substances to be found naturally in all three states on earth. Water takes many different forms on Earth: water vapor and clouds in the sky; seawater and rarely icebergs in the ocean; glaciers and rivers in the mountains; and the liquid in aquifers in the ground.

Water can dissolve many different substances, giving it different tastes and odours. In fact, humans and other animals have developed senses which are, to a degree, able to evaluate the potability of water, avoiding water that is too salty or putrid. Humans also tend to prefer cold water to lukewarm; cold water is likely to contain fewer microbes. The taste advertised in spring water or mineral water derives from the minerals dissolved in it, as pure H_2O is tasteless. As such, purity in spring and mineral water refers to purity from toxins, pollutants, and microbes.

Different names are given to water's various forms:

- Solid - ice

- Siquid - water
- Gaseous - water vapour

According to meteorology:

- Hydrometeor
- Precipitation

Precipitation according to moves vertical (falling) precipitation:

- Rain
- Freezing rain
- Drizzle
- Freezing drizzle
- Snow
- Snow pellets
- Snow grains
- Ice pellets
- Frozen rain
- Hail
- Ice crystals
- Horizontal (seated) precipitation
- Dew
- Hoarfrost
- Atmospheric icing
- Glaze ice

Precipitation according to state:

- Liquid precipitation
- Rain
- Freezing rain
- Drizzle
- Freezing drizzle
- Dew
- Solid precipitation
- Snow
- Snow pellets
- Snow grains
- Ice pellets
- Frozen rain
- Hail
- Ice crystals
- Hoarfrost
- Atmospheric icing
- Glaze ice
- Mixed precipitation
- In temperatures around 0 °C
- Levitating particles
- Clouds
- Fog

- Mist
- Ascending particles (drifted by wind)
- Spindrift
- Stirred snow

According to occurrence:

- Groundwater
- Meltwater
- Meteoric water
- Connate water
- Fresh water
- Surface water
- Mineral water – contains much minerals
- Brackish water
- Dead water – strange phenomenon which can occur when a layer of fresh or brackish water rests on top of denser salt water, without the two layers mixing. It is dangerous for ship traveling.
- seawater
- Brine

According to uses:

- Tap water
- Bottled water
- Drinking water or potable water – useful for everyday drinking, without fouling, it contains balanced minerals that are not harmful to health.

Purified water, laboratory-grade, analytical-grade or reagent-grade water – water which has been highly purified for specific uses in science or engineering. Often broadly classified as Type I, Type II, or Type III, this category of water includes, but is not limited to the following:

- Distilled water
- Double distilled water
- Deionized water

According to other features:

- Soft water – contains less minerals
- Hard water – from underground, contains more minerals
- Distilled water, double distilled water, deionized water - contains no minerals.
- Water of crystallization – water incorporated into crystalline structures.
- Hydrates – water bound into other chemical substances.
- Heavy water – made from heavy atoms of hydrogen - deuterium. It is in nature in normal water in very low concentration. It was used in construction of first nuclear reactors.
- Tritiated water

According to microbiology:

- Drinking water
- Wastewater
- Storm water or surface water

According to religion:

- Holy water

Chemical and Physical Properties

Water is the chemical substance with chemical formula H_2O: one molecule of water has two hydrogen atoms covalently bonded to a single oxygen atom. The major chemical and physical properties of water are:

- Water is a tasteless, odorless liquid at ambient temperature and pressure. The color of water and ice is, intrinsically, a very light blue hue, although water appears colorless in small quantities. Ice also appears colorless, and water vapor is essentially invisible as a gas.

- Water is transparent, and thus aquatic plants can live within the water because sunlight can reach them. Only strong UV light is slightly absorbed.

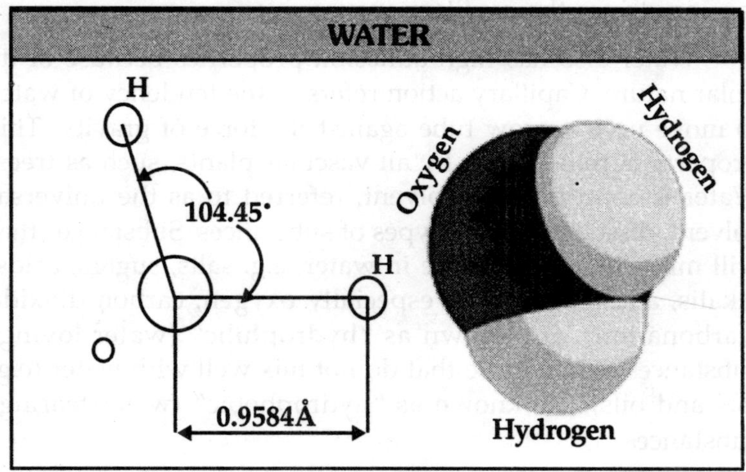

Fig. 2.1

Water is necessary solvent for all known life and an abundant compound on the earth's surface

Since oxygen has a higher electronegativity than hydrogen, water is a polar molecule. The oxygen has a slight negative charge while the hydrogens have a slight positive charge giving the article a strong effective dipole moment. The interactions between the different dipoles of each molecule cause a net attraction force associated with water's high amount of surface tension.

Another very important force that causes the water molecules to stick to one another is the hydrogen bond.

The boiling point of water (and all other liquids) is directly related to the barometric pressure. For example, on the top of Mt. Everest water boils at about 68 °C (154 °F), compared to 100 °C (212 °F) at sea level. Conversely, water deep in the ocean near geothermal vents can reach temperatures of hundreds of degrees and remain liquid.

Water has a high surface tension caused by the weak interactions, (Van Der Waals Force) between water molecules because it is polar. The apparent elasticity caused by surface tension drives the capillary waves.

Water also has high adhesion properties because of its polar nature. Capillary action refers to the tendency of water to move up a narrow tube against the force of gravity. This property is relied upon by all vascular plants, such as trees. Water is a very strong solvent, referred to as the universal solvent, dissolving many types of substances. Substances that will mix well and dissolve in water, e.g. salts, sugars, acids, alkalis, and some gases: especially oxygen, carbon dioxide (carbonation), are known as "hydrophilic" (water-loving) substances, while those that do not mix well with water (e.g. fats and oils), are known as "hydrophobic" (water-fearing) substances.

All the major components in cells (proteins, DNA and polysaccharides) are also dissolved in water. Pure water has a low electrical conductivity, but this increases significantly upon solvation of a small amount of ionic material such as sodium chloride. Water has the second highest specific heat capacity of any known chemical compound, after ammonia, as well as a high heat of vaporization (40.65 kJ mol-1), both of which are a result of the extensive hydrogen bonding between its molecules. These two unusual properties allow water to moderate Earth's climate by buffering large fluctuations in temperature.

The maximum density of water is at 3.98 °C (39.16 °F) Water becomes even less dense upon freezing, expanding 9%. This causes an unusual phenomenon: ice floats upon water, and so water organisms can live inside a partly frozen pond because the water on the bottom has a temperature of around 4 °C (39 °F).

Water is miscible with many liquids, for example ethanol, in all proportions, forming a single homogeneous liquid. On the other hand, water and most oils are immiscible usually forming layers according to increasing density from the top. As a gas, water vapor is completely miscible with air. Water forms an azeotrope with many other solvents. Water can be split by electrolysis into hydrogen and oxygen.

As an oxide of hydrogen, water is formed when hydrogen or hydrogen-containing compounds burn or react with oxygen or oxygen-containing compounds. Water is not a fuel, it is an end-product of the combustion of hydrogen. The energy required to split water into hydrogen and oxygen by electrolysis or any other means is greater than the energy.

Elements which are more electropositive than hydrogen such as lithium, sodium, calcium, potassium and caesium displace hydrogen from water, forming hydroxides. Being a flammable gas, the hydrogen given off is dangerous and the reaction of water with the more electropositive of these elements is violently explosive.

DISTRIBUTION OF WATER IN NATURE

Water in the Universe

Much of the universe's water may be produced as a by-product of star formation. When stars are born, their birth is accompanied by a strong outward wind of gas and dust. When this outflow of material eventually impacts the surrounding gas, the shock waves that are created compress and heat the gas. The water observed is quickly produced in this warm dense gas.

Water has been detected in interstellar clouds within our galaxy, the Milky Way. It is believed that water exists in abundance in other galaxies too, because its components, hydrogen and oxygen, are among the most abundant elements in the universe. Interstellar clouds eventually condense into solar nebulae and solar systems, such as ours.

Water vapour is present on:

- Mercury - 3.4% in the atmosphere, and large amounts of water in Mercury's exosphere
- Venus - 0.002% in the atmosphere
- Earth - trace in the atmosphere (varies with climate)
- Mars - 0.03% in the atmosphere
- Jupiter - 0.0004% in the atmosphere
- Saturn - in ices only
- Enceladus (moon of Saturn) - 91% in the atmosphere exoplanets known as HD 189733 b and HD 209458 b

Liquid water is present on:

- Earth - 71% of surface
- Moon - small amounts of water have been found (in 2008) in the inside of volcanic pearls brought from Moon to Earth by the Apollo 15 crew in 1971.

Strong evidence suggests that liquid water is present just under the surface of Saturn's moon Enceladus. There is probably some liquid water on Europa.

Water ice is present on:

- Earth - mainly on ice sheets
- Polar ice caps on Mars
- Titan
- Europa
- Enceladus

Probability or possibility of distribution of water ice is at: lunar ice on the Moon, Ceres (dwarf planet), Tethys (moon). Ice is probably in internal structure of Uranus, Neptune, and Pluto and on comets.

Water and Habitable Zone

The existence of liquid water, and to a lesser extent its gaseous and solid forms, on Earth is vital to the existence of life on Earth as we know it. The Earth is located in the habitable zone of the solar system; if it were slightly closer to or further from the Sun (about 5%, or about 8 million kilometres), the conditions which allow the three forms to be present simultaneously would be far less likely to exist.

Earth's mass allows gravity to hold an atmosphere. Water vapor and carbon dioxide in the atmosphere provide a greenhouse effect which helps maintain a relatively steady surface temperature. If Earth were smaller, a thinner atmosphere would cause temperature extremes preventing the accumulation of water except in polar ice caps (as on Mars).

It has been proposed that life itself may maintain the conditions that have allowed its continued existence. The surface temperature of Earth has been relatively constant through geologic time despite varying levels of incoming solar radiation (insolation), indicating that a dynamic process governs Earth's temperature via a combination of greenhouse gases and surface or atmospheric albedo. This proposal is known as the Gaia hypothesis.

The state of water also depends on a planet's gravity. If a planet is sufficiently massive, the water on it may be solid even at high temperatures, because of the high pressure caused by gravity. There are various theories about origin of water on Earth.

Water on Earth

Hydrology is the study of the movement, distribution, and quality of water throughout the Earth. The study of the distribution of water is hydrography. The study of the distribution and movement of groundwater is hydrogeology, of glaciers is glaciology, of inland waters is limnology and distribution of oceans is oceanography. Ecological processes with hydrology are in focus of ecohydrology.

The collective mass of water found on, under, and over the surface of a planet is called the hydrosphere. Earth's approximate water volume (the total water supply of the world) is 1 360 000 000 km³ (326 000 000 mi³). Of this volume:

- 1320 000 000 km³ (316 900 000 mi³ or 97.2%) is in the oceans.
- 25 000 000 km³ (6 000 000 mi³ or 1.8%) is in glaciers, ice caps and ice sheets.
- 13 000 000 km³ (3,000,000 mi³ or 0.9%) is groundwater.
- 250 000 km³ (60,000 mi³ or 0.02%) is fresh water in lakes, inland seas, and rivers.
- 13 000 km³ (3,100 mi³ or 0.001%) is atmospheric water vapor at any given time.

Groundwater and fresh water are useful or potentially useful to humans as water resources.

Liquid water is found in bodies of water, such as an ocean, sea, lake, river, stream, canal, pond, or puddle. The majority of water on Earth is sea water. Water is also present in the atmosphere in solid, liquid, and vapor states. It also exists as groundwater in aquifers.

The most important geological processes caused by water are:

- chemical weathering;
- water erosion;
- water sediment transport and sedimentation, mudflows, ice erosion and sedimentation by glacier.

Water Cycle

The water cycle (known scientifically as the hydrologic cycle) refers to the continuous exchange of water within the hydrosphere, between the atmosphere, soil water, surface water, groundwater, and plants.

Water moves perpetually through each of these regions in the water cycle consisting of following transfer processes:

- evaporation from oceans and other water bodies into the air and transpiration from land plants and animals into air.
- precipitation, from water vapor condensing from the air and falling to earth or ocean.
- runoff from the land usually reaching the sea.

Most water vapour over the oceans returns to the oceans, but winds carry water vapour over land at the same rate as runoff into the sea, about 36 Tt per year. Over land, evaporation and transpiration contribute another 71 Tt per year. Precipitation, at a rate of 107 Tt per year over land, has several forms: most commonly rain, snow, and hail, with some contribution from fog and dew. Condensed water in the air may also refract sunlight to produce rainbows.

Water runoff often collects over watersheds flowing into rivers. A mathematical model used to simulate river or stream flow and calculate water quality parameters is hydrological transport model. Some of water is diverted to irrigation for agriculture. Rivers and seas offer opportunity for travel and commerce. Through erosion, runoff shapes the environment creating river valleys and deltas which provide rich soil and level ground for the establishment of population centers. A flood occurs when an area of land, usually low-lying, is covered with water. It is when a river overflows its banks or flood from the sea. A drought is an extended period of months or years when a region notes a deficiency in its water supply. This occurs when a region receives consistently below average precipitation.

Fresh Water Storage

Some runoff water is trapped for periods, for example in lakes. At high altitude, during winter, and in the far north and south, snow collects in ice caps, snow pack and glaciers. Water also infiltrates the ground and goes into aquifers. This groundwater later flows back to the surface in springs, or more spectacularly in hot springs and geysers. Groundwater is also extracted artificially in wells. This water storage is important, since clean, fresh water is essential to human and other land-based life. In many parts of the world, it is in short supply.

Tides

Tides are the cyclic rising and falling of Earth's ocean surface caused by the tidal forces of the Moon and the Sun acting on the oceans. Tides cause changes in the depth of the marine and estuarine water bodies and produce oscillating currents known as tidal streams. The changing tide produced at a given location is the result of the changing positions of the Moon and Sun relative to the Earth coupled with the effects of Earth rotation and the local bathymetry. The strip of seashore that is submerged at high tide and exposed at low tide, the intertidal zone, is an important ecological product of ocean tides.

Effects on Life

From a biological standpoint, water has many distinct properties that are critical for the proliferation of life that set it apart from other substances. It carries out this role by allowing organic compounds to react in ways that ultimately allow replication. All known forms of life depend on water. Water is vital both as a solvent in which many of the body's solutes dissolve and as an essential part of many metabolic processes within the body. Metabolism is the sum total of anabolism and catabolism. In anabolism, water is removed from molecules (through energy requiring enzymatic chemical reactions) in order to grow larger molecules (e.g. starches, triglycerides and proteins for storage of fuels and information). In catabolism, water is used to break bonds in order to generate smaller molecules (e.g. glucose, fatty acids and amino acids to be used for fuels for energy use or other purposes). Water is thus essential and central to these metabolic processes. Therefore, without water, these metabolic processes would cease to exist, leaving us to muse about what processes would be in its place, such as gas absorption, dust collection, etc.

Water is also central to photosynthesis and respiration. Photosynthetic cells use the sun's energy to split off water's hydrogen from oxygen. Hydrogen is combined with CO_2 (absorbed from air or water) to form glucose and release oxygen. All living cells use such fuels and oxidize the hydrogen and carbon to capture the sun's energy and reform water and CO_2 in the process (cellular respiration).

Water is also central to acid-base neutrality and enzyme function. An acid, a hydrogen ion (H^+, that is, a proton) donor, can be neutralized by a base, a proton acceptor such as hydroxide ion (OH^-) to form water. Water is considered to be neutral, with a pH (the negative log of the hydrogen ion concentration) of 7. Acids have pH values less than 7 while bases have values greater than 7. Stomach acid (HCl) is useful to digestion. However, its corrosive effect on the esophagus during reflux can temporarily be neutralized by ingestion of a base such as aluminum hydroxide to produce the neutral molecules water and the salt aluminum chloride. Human biochemistry that involves enzymes usually performs optimally around a biologically neutral pH of 7.4.

For example a cell of Escherichia coli contains 70% of water, a human body 60-70%, plant body up to 90% and the body of an adult jellyfish is made up of 94-98% water.

Aquatic Life Forms

Earth's waters are filled with life. The earliest life forms appeared in water; nearly all fish live exclusively in water, and there are many types of marine mammals, such as dolphins and whales that also live in the water. Some kinds of animals, such as amphibians, spend portions of their lives in water and portions on land. Plants such as kelp and algae grow in the water and are the basis for some underwater ecosystems. Plankton is generally the foundation of the ocean food chain.

Aquatic animals must obtain oxygen to survive, and they do so in various ways. Fish have gills instead of lungs, although some species of fish, such as the lungfish, have both. Marine mammals, such as dolphins, whales, otters, and seals need to surface periodically to breathe air. Smaller life forms are able to absorb oxygen through their skin.

Effects on Human Civilization

Civilization has historically flourished around rivers and major waterways; Mesopotamia, the so-called cradle of civilization, was situated between the major rivers Tigris and Euphrates; the ancient society of the Egyptians depended entirely upon the Nile. Large metropolises like Rotterdam, London, Montreal, Paris, New York City, Buenos Aires, Shanghai, Tokyo, Chicago, and Hong Kong owe their success in part to their easy accessibility via water and the resultant expansion of trade. Islands with safe water ports, like Singapore, have flourished for the same reason. In places such as North Africa and the Middle East, where water is more scarce, access to clean drinking water was and is a major factor in human development.

Health and Pollution

Water fit for human consumption is called drinking water or potable water. Water that is not potable can be made potable by filtration or distillation (heating it until it becomes water vapor, and then capturing the vapor without any of the impurities it leaves behind), or by other methods (chemical or heat treatment that kills bacteria). Sometimes the term safe water is applied to potable water of a lower quality threshold (i.e., it is used effectively for nutrition in humans that have weak access to water cleaning processes, and does more good than harm). Water that is not fit for drinking but is not harmful for humans when used for swimming or bathing is called by various names other than potable or drinking water, and is sometimes called safe water, or "safe for bathing". Chlorine is a skin and mucous membrane irritant that is used to make water safe for bathing or drinking. Its use is highly technical and is usually monitored by government regulations (typically 1 part per million (ppm) for drinking water, and 1-2 ppm of chlorine not yet reacted with impurities for bathing water).

This natural resource is becoming scarcer in certain places, and its availability is a major social and economic concern. Currently, about 1 billion people around the world routinely drink unhealthy water. Most countries accepted the goal of halving by 2015 the number of people worldwide who do not have access to safe water and sanitation during the 2003 G8 Evian summit Even if this difficult goal is met, it will still leave more than an estimated half a billion people without access to safe drinking water and over 1 billion without access to adequate sanitation. Poor water quality and bad sanitation are deadly; some 5 million deaths a year are caused by polluted drinking water. The World Health Organization estimates that safe water could prevent 1.4 million child deaths from diarrhea each year Water, however, is not a finite resource, but rather re-circulated as potable water in precipitation in quantities many degrees of magnitude higher than human consumption. Therefore, it is the relatively small quantity of water in reserve in the earth (about 1% of our drinking water supply, which is replenished in aquifers around every 1 to 10 years), that is a nonrenewable resource, and it is, rather, the distribution of potable and irrigation water which is scarce, rather than the actual amount of it that exists on the earth. Water-poor countries use importation of goods as the primary method of importing water (to leave enough for local human consumption), since the manufacturing process uses around 10 to 100 times products' masses in water.

In the developing world, 90% of all wastewater still goes untreated into local rivers and streams Some 50 countries, with roughly a third of the world's population, also suffer from medium or high water stress, and 17 of these extract more water annually than is recharged through their natural water cycles The strain not only affects surface freshwater bodies like rivers and lakes, but it also degrades groundwater resources.

HUMAN USES

Agriculture

The most important use of water in agriculture is for an irrigation and irrigation is key component to produce enough food. Irrigation takes up to 90% of water withdrawn in some developing countries.

As a Scientific Standard

On 7 April 1795, the gram was defined in France to be equal to "the absolute weight of a volume of pure water equal to a cube of one hundredth of a meter, and to the temperature of the melting ice." For practical purposes though, a metallic reference standard was required, one thousand times more massive, the kilogram. Work was therefore commissioned to determine precisely how massive one liter of water was. In spite of the fact that the decreed definition of the gram specified water at 0 °C—a highly stable temperature point—the scientists chose to redefine the standard and to perform their measurements at the most stable density point: the temperature at which water reaches maximum density, which was measured at the time as 4 °C.

The Kelvin temperature scale of the SI system is based on the triple point of water, defined as exactly 273.16 K or 0.01 °C. The scale is a more accurate development of the Celsius temperature scale, which is defined by the boiling point (100 °C) and melting point (0 °C) of water.

Natural water consists mainly of the isotopes hydrogen-1 and oxygen-16, but there is also small quantity of heavier isotopes such as hydrogen-2 (deuterium). The amount of deuterium oxides or heavy water is very small, but it still affects the properties of water. Water from rivers and lakes tends to contain less deuterium than seawater. Therefore, a standard water called Vienna Standard Mean Ocean Water is defined as the standard water.

For Drinking

The human body is anywhere from 55% to 78% water depending on body size to function properly, the body requires between one and seven liters of water per day to avoid dehydration; the precise amount depends on the level of activity, temperature, humidity, and other factors. Most of this is ingested through foods or beverages other than drinking straight water. It is not clear how much water intake is needed by healthy people, though most advocates agree that 6-7 glasses of water (approximately 2 litres) daily is the minimum to maintain proper hydration Medical literature favors a lower consumption, typically 1 litre of water for an average male, excluding extra requirements due to fluid loss from exercise or warm weather. For those who have healthy kidneys, it is rather difficult to drink too much water, but (especially in warm humid weather and while exercising) it is dangerous to drink too little. People can drink far more water than necessary while exercising, however, putting them at risk of water intoxication (hyperhydration), which can be fatal. The "fact" that a person should consume eight glasses of water per day cannot be traced back to a scientific source. There are other myths such as the effect of water on weight loss and constipation that have been dispelled.

An original recommendation for water intake in 1945 by the Food and Nutrition Board of the National Research Council read: "An ordinary standard for diverse persons is 1 milliliter for each calorie of food. Most of this quantity is contained in prepared foods." The latest dietary reference intake report by the United States National Research Council in general recommended (including food sources): 2.7 litres of water total for women and 3.7 litres for men Specifically, pregnant and breast-feeding women need additional fluids to stay hydrated. According to the Institute of Medicine—who recommend that, on average, women consume 2.2 litres and men 3.0 litres—this is recommended to be 2.4 litres (approx. 9 cups) for pregnant women and 3 litres (approx. 12.5 cups) for breast-feeding women since an especially large amount of fluid is lost during nursing Also noted is that normally, about 20 per cent of water intake comes from food, while the rest comes from drinking water and beverages (caffeinated included). Water is excreted from the body in multiple forms; through urine and feces, through sweating, and by exhalation of water vapor in the breath. With physical exertion and heat exposure, water loss will increase and daily fluid needs may increase as well.

Humans require water that does not contain too many impurities. Common impurities include metal salts and/or harmful bacteria, such as Vibrio. Some solutes are acceptable and even desirable for taste enhancement and to provide needed electrolytes.

The single largest freshwater resource suitable for drinking is Lake Baikal in Siberia, which has a very low salt and calcium content and is very clean.

As a Dissolving Agent or Solvent

Dissolving (or suspending) is used to wash everyday items such as the human body, clothes, floors, cars, food, and pets. Also, human wastes are carried by water in the sewage system. Its use as a cleaning solvent consumes most of water in industrialized countries.

Water can facilitate the chemical processing of wastewater. An aqueous environment can be favourable to the breakdown of pollutants, due to the ability to gain an homogenous solution that is pumpable and flexible to treat. Aerobic treatment can be used by applying oxygen or air to a solution reduce the reactivity of substances within it.

Water also facilitates biological processing of waste that have been dissolved within it. Micro-organisms that live within water can access dissolved wastes and can feed upon them breaking them down into less polluting substances. Reedbeds and anaerobic digesters are both examples of biological systems that are particularly suited to the treatment of effluents.

Typically from both chemical and biological treatment of wastes, there is often a solid residue or cake that is left over from the treatment process. Depending upon its constituent parts, this 'cake' may be dried and spread on land as a fertilizer if it has beneficial properties, or alternatively disposed of in landfill or incinerated.

As a Heat Transfer Fluid

Water and steam are used as heat transfer fluids in diverse heat exchange systems, due to its availability and high heat capacity, both as a coolant and for heating. Cool water may even be naturally available from a lake or the sea. Condensing steam is a particularly efficient heating fluid because of the large heat of vapourization. A disadvantage is that water and steam are somewhat corrosive. In almost all electric power plants, water is the coolant, which vaporizes and drives steam turbines to drive generators.

In the nuclear industry, water can also be used as a neutron moderator. In a pressurized water reactor, water is both a coolant and a moderator. This provides a passive safety measure, as removing the water from the reactor also slows the nuclear reaction down.

Extinguishing Fires

Water is used for fighting wildfires. Water has a high heat of vapourization and is relatively inert, which makes it a good fire extinguishing fluid. The evapouration of water carries heat away from the fire. However, water cannot be used to fight fires of electric equipment, because impure water is electrically conductive, or of oils and organic solvents, because they float on water and the explosive boiling of water tends to spread the burning liquid.

Use of water in fire fighting should also take into account the hazards of a steam explosion, which may occur when water is used on very hot fires in confined spaces, and of a hydrogen explosion, when substances which react with water, such as certain metals or hot graphite, decompose the water, producing hydrogen gas.

The power of such explosions was seen in the Chernobyl disaster, although the water involved did not come from fire-fighting at that time but the reactor's own water cooling system. A steam explosion occurred when the extreme over-heating of the core caused water to flash into steam. A hydrogen explosion may have occurred as a result of reaction between steam and hot zirconium.

Chemical Uses

Organic reactions are usually quenched with water or a water solution of a suitable acid, base or buffer. Water is generally effective in removing inorganic salts. In inorganic reactions, water is a common solvent. In organic reactions, it is usually not used as a reaction solvent, because it does not dissolve the reactants well and is amphoteric (acidic and basic) and nucleophilic. Nevertheless, these properties are sometimes desirable. Also, acceleration of Diels-Alder reactions by water has been observed. Supercritical water has recently been a topic of research. Oxygen-saturated supercritical water combusts organic pollutants efficiently.

Recreation

Humans use water for many recreational purposes, as well as for exercising and for sports. Some of these include swimming, water-skiing, boating, and diving. In addition, some sports, like ice hockey and ice skating, are played on ice. Lakesides, beaches and waterparks are popular places for people to go to relax and enjoy recreation. Many find the sound of flowing water to be calming, too. Some keep fish and other life in aquariums or ponds for show, fun, and companionship. Humans also use water for snow sports i.e. skiing or snowboarding, which requires the water to be frozen. People may also use water for play fighting such as with snowballs, water guns or water balloons. They may also make fountains and use water in their public or private decorations.

Water Industry

The water industry provides drinking water and wastewater services (including sewage treatment) to households and industry.

Water used in landscaping. Water supply facilities includes for example water wells cisterns for rainwater harvesting, water supply network, water purification facilities, water tanks, water towers, water pipes including old aqueducts. Atmospheric water generator is in development.

Drinking water is often collected at springs, extracted from artificial borings in the ground, or wells. Building more wells in adequate places is thus a possible way to produce more water, assuming the aquifers can supply an adequate flow. Other water sources are rainwater and river or lake water. This surface water, however, must be purified for human consumption. This may involve removal of undissolved substances, dissolved substances and harmful microbes. Popular methods are filtering with sand which only removes undissolved material, while chlorination and boiling kill harmful microbes. Distillation does all three functions. More advanced techniques exist, such as reverse osmosis. Desalination of abundant ocean or seawater is a more expensive solution used in coastal arid climates.

The distribution of drinking water is done through municipal water systems or as bottled water. Governments in many countries have programs to distribute water to the needy at no charge. Others argue that the market mechanism and free enterprise are best to manage this rare resource and to finance the boring of wells or the construction of dams and reservoirs.

Reducing waste by using drinking water only for human consumption is another option. In some cities such as Hong Kong, sea water is extensively used for flushing toilets citywide in order to conserve fresh water resources.

Polluting water may be the biggest single misuse of water; to the extent that a pollutant limits other uses of the water, it becomes a waste of the resource, regardless of benefits to the polluter. Like other types of pollution, this does not enter standard accounting of market costs, being conceived as externalities for which the market cannot account. Thus other people pay the price of water pollution, while the private firms' profits are not redistributed to the local population victim of this pollution. Pharmaceuticals consumed by humans often end up in the waterways and can have detrimental effects on aquatic life if they bioaccumulate and if they are not biodegradable.

Wastewater facilities are sewers and wastewater treatment plants. Another way to remove pollution from surface runoff water is bioswale.

Industrial Applications

Water is used in power generation. Hydroelectricity is electricity obtained from hydropower. Hydroelectric power comes from water driving a water turbine connected to a generator. Hydroelectricity is a low-cost, non-polluting, renewable energy source. The energy is supplied by the sun. Heat from the sun evaporates water, which condenses as rain in higher altitudes, from where it flows down.

Pressurized water is used in water blasting and water jet cutters. Also, very high pressure water guns are used for precise cutting. It works very well, is relatively safe, and is not harmful to the environment. It is also used in the cooling of machinery to prevent over-heating, or prevent saw blades from over-heating.

Water is also used in many industrial processes and machines, such as the steam turbine and heat exchanger, in addition to its use as a chemical solvent. Discharge of untreated water from industrial uses is pollution. Pollution includes discharged solutes (chemical pollution) and discharged coolant water (thermal pollution). Industry requires pure water for many applications and utilizes a variety of purification techniques both in water supply and discharge.

Food Processing

Water plays many critical roles within the field of food science. It is important for a food scientist to understand the roles that water plays within food processing to ensure the success of their products.

Solutes such as salts and sugars found in water affect the physical properties of water. The boiling and freezing points of water is affected by solutes. One mole of sucrose (sugar) raises the boiling point of water by 0.52 °C, and one mole of salt raises the boiling point by 1.04 °C while lowering the freezing point of water in a similar way Solutes in water also affect water activity which affects many chemical reactions and the growth of microbes in food Water activity can be described as a ratio of the vapor pressure of water in a solution to the vapor pressure of pure water Solutes in water lower water activity. This is important to know because most bacterial growth ceases at low levels of water activity. Not only does microbial growth affect the safety of food but also the preservation and shelf life of food.

Water hardness is also a critical factor in food processing. It can dramatically affect the quality of a product as well as playing a role in sanitation. Water hardness is classified based on the amounts of removable calcium carbonate salt it contains per gallon. Water hardness is measured in grains; 0.064 g calcium carbonate is equivalent to one grain of hardness Water is classified as soft if it contains 1 to 4 grains, medium if it contains 5 to 10 grains and hard if it contains 11 to 20 grains. The hardness of water may be altered or treated by using a chemical ion exchange system. The hardness of water also affects its pH balance which plays a critical role in food processing. For example, hard water prevents successful production of clear beverages. Water hardness also affects sanitation; with increasing hardness, there is a loss of effectiveness for its use as a sanitizer.

Boiling, steaming, and simmering are popular cooking methods that often require immersing food in water or its gaseous state, steam. While cooking water is used for dishwashing too.

3 Water Molecule and its Properties

Water (H_2O, HOH) is the most abundant molecule on Earth's surface, composing of about 70% of the Earth's surface as liquid and solid state in addition to being found in the atmosphere as a vapor. It is in dynamic equilibrium between the liquid and gas states at standard temperature and pressure. At room temperature, it is a nearly colorless (with a hint of blue), tasteless, and odorless liquid. Many substances dissolve in water and it is commonly referred to as the universal solvent. Because of this, water in nature and in use is rarely pure, and may have some properties different from those in the laboratory. However, there are many compounds that are essentially, if not completely, insoluble in water. Water is the only common substance found naturally in all three common states of matter—for other substances, see Chemical properties. Water is essential for all life on Earth. Water also usually makes up 55% to 78% of the human body.

Water can take many forms. The solid state of water is known as ice; the gaseous state is known as water vapour (or steam), and the common liquid phase is generally taken as simply water. Above a certain critical temperature and pressure (47 K and 22.064?MPa), water molecules assume a supercritical condition, in which liquid-like clusters float within a vapour-like phase.

Heavy water is water in which the hydrogen is replaced by its heavier isotope, deuterium. It is chemically almost identical to normal water. Heavy water is used in the nuclear industry to slow down neutrons.

Physics and Chemistry of Water

Water is the chemical substance with chemical formula H_2O: one molecule of water has two hydrogen atoms covalently bonded to a single oxygen atom. Water is a tasteless, odorless liquid at ambient temperature and pressure, and appears colorless in small quantities, although it has its own intrinsic very light blue hue. Ice also appears colorless, and water vapor is essentially invisible as a gas. Water is primarily a liquid under standard conditions, which is not predicted from its relationship to other analogous hydrides of the oxygen family in the periodic table, which are gases such as hydrogen sulfide. Also the elements surrounding oxygen in the periodic table, nitrogen, fluorine, phosphorus, sulfur and chlorine, all combine with hydrogen to produce gases under standard conditions. The reason that water forms a liquid is that it is more electronegative than all of these elements (other than fluorine). Oxygen attracts electrons much more strongly than hydrogen, resulting in a net positive charge on the hydrogen atoms, and a net negative charge on the oxygen atom. The presence of a charge on each of these atoms gives each water molecule a net dipole moment. Electrical attraction between water molecules due to this dipole pulls individual molecules closer together, making it more difficult to separate the molecules and therefore raising the boiling point. This attraction is known as hydrogen bonding. Water can be described as a polar liquid that dissociates disproportionately into the hydronium ion [H_3O^+(aq)] and an associated hydroxide ion [OH^-(aq)]. Water is in dynamic equilibrium between the liquid, gas and solid states at standard temperature and pressure (0 °C, 100.000 kPa) and is the only pure substance found naturally on Earth to be so.

Water, Ice and Vapour

Water has the second highest specific heat capacity of any known chemical compound, after ammonia, as well as a high heat of vapourization (40.65 kJ mol^{-1}), both of which are a result of the extensive hydrogen bonding between its molecules. These two unusual properties allow water to moderate Earth's climate by buffering large fluctuations in temperature.

The specific enthalpy of fusion of water is 333.55 kJ kg^{-1} at 0 °C. Of common substances, only that of ammonia is higher. This property confers resistance to melting upon the ice of glaciers and drift ice. Before the advent of mechanical refrigeration, ice was in common use to retard food spoilage.

Density of Water and Ice

The solid form of most substances is more dense than the liquid phase; thus, a block of pure solid substance will sink in a tub of pure liquid substance. But, by contrast, a block of common ice will float in a tub of water because solid water is less dense than liquid water. This is an extremely important property of water. At room temperature, liquid water becomes denser with lowering temperature, just like other substances. But at 4 °C (3.98 to be precise), just above freezing, water reaches its maximum density, and as water cools further toward its freezing point, the liquid water, under standard conditions, expands to become less dense. The physical reason for this is related to the crystal structure of ordinary ice, known as hexagonal ice (Ih). Water, lead, uranium, neon and silicon are some of the few materials which expand when they freeze; most other materials contract. Not all forms of ice are less dense than liquid water however, HDA and VHDA for example are both denser than liquid phase pure water. Thus, the reason that the common form of ice is less dense than water is somewhat non-intuitive and relies heavily on the unusual properties inherent to the hydrogen bond.

Generally, water expands when it freezes because of its molecular structure, in tandem with the unusual elasticity of the hydrogen bond and the particular lowest energy hexagonal crystal conformation that it adopts under standard conditions. That is, when water cools, it tries to stack in a crystalline lattice configuration that stretches the rotational and vibrational components of the bond. Although the H⁻ bond length is actually shorter in solid ice than between molecules of liquid water, the rigidity of the ice crystalline structure ensures that each given H_2O molecule has fewer neighbors, and thus the solid is less dense. This effectively reduces the density of water when ice is formed under standard conditions.

Water shares the higher-density liquid state with only a few materials like gallium, germanium, bismuth and antimony.

The importance of this property cannot be overemphasized for its role on the ecosystem of Earth. For example, if water were denser when frozen, lakes and oceans in a polar environment would eventually freeze solid. This would happen because frozen ice would settle on the lake and riverbeds, and the necessary warming phenomenon could not occur in summer, as the warm surface layer would be less dense than the solid frozen layer below. It is a significant feature of nature that this does not occur naturally in the environment.

Nevertheless, the unusual expansion of freezing water (in ordinary natural settings in relevant biological systems), due to the hydrogen bond, from 4 °C above freezing to the freezing point offers an important advantage for freshwater life in winter. Water chilled at the surface increases in density and sinks, forming convection currents that cool the whole water body, but when the temperature of the lake water reaches 4 °C, water on the surface decreases in density as it chills further and remains as a surface layer which eventually freezes and forms ice. Since downward convection of colder water is blocked by the density change, any large body of fresh water frozen in winter will have the coldest water near the surface, away from the riverbed or lakebed.

Water will freeze at 0 °C (32 °F, 273 K), however, it can be supercooled in a fluid state down to its crystal homogeneous nucleation at almost 231 K (-42 °C)

Water expands significantly as the temperature increases. The density is 4% less than maximum as the temperature approaches boiling.

Density of Saltwater and Ice

The density of water is dependent on the dissolved salt content as well as the temperature of the water. Ice still floats in the oceans, otherwise they would freeze from the bottom up. However, the salt content of oceans lowers the freezing point by about 2 °C and lowers the temperature of the density maximum of water to the freezing point. That is why, in ocean water, the downward convection of colder water is not blocked by an expansion of water as it becomes colder near the freezing point. The oceans' cold water near the freezing point continues to sink. For this reason, any creature attempting to survive at the bottom of such cold water as the Arctic Ocean generally lives in water that is 4 °C colder than the temperature at the bottom of frozen-over fresh water lakes and rivers in the winter.

As the surface of salt water begins to freeze (at -1.9 °C for normal salinity seawater, 3.5%) the ice that forms is essentially salt free with a density approximately equal to that of freshwater ice. This ice floats on the surface and the salt that is "frozen out" adds to the salinity and density of the seawater just below it, in a process known as brine rejection. This denser saltwater sinks by convection and the replacing seawater is subject to the same process. This provides essentially freshwater ice at -1.9 °C on the surface. The increased density of the seawater beneath the forming ice causes it to sink towards the bottom. On a large scale, the process of brine rejection and sinking cold salty water results in ocean currents forming to transport such water away from the pole. One potential consequence of global warming is that the loss of Arctic ice could result in the loss of these currents as well, which could have unforeseeable consequences on near and distant climates.

Miscibility and Condensation

Water is miscible with many liquids, for example ethanol in all proportions, forming a single homogeneous liquid. On the other hand water and most oils are immiscible usually forming layers according to increasing density from the top.

As a gas, water vapor is completely miscible with air. On the other hand the maximum water vapor pressure that is thermodynamically stable with the liquid (or solid) at a given temperature is relatively low compared with total atmospheric pressure. For example, if the vapor partial pressure is 2% of atmospheric pressure and the air is cooled from 25 °C, starting at about 22 °C water will start to condense, defining the dew point, and creating fog or dew. The reverse process accounts for the fog burning off in the morning. If one raises the humidity at room temperature, say by running a hot shower or a bath, and the temperature stays about the same, the vapor soon reaches the pressure for phase change, and condenses out as steam. A gas in this context is referred to as saturated or 100% relative humidity, when the vapor pressure of water in the air is at the equilibrium with vapor pressure due to (liquid) water; water (or ice, if cool enough) will fail to lose mass through evaporation when exposed to saturated air. Because the amount of water vapor in air is small, relative humidity, the ratio of the partial pressure due to the water vapor to the saturated partial vapor pressure, is much more useful. Water vapor pressure above 100% relative humidity is called super-saturated and can occur if air is rapidly cooled, say by rising suddenly in an updraft.

VAPOUR PRESSURES OF WATER

Compressibility

The compressibility of water is a function of pressure and temperature. At 0 °C in the limit of zero pressure the compressibility is $5.1 \times 10^{-5}\ P_a^{-1}$. In the zero pressure limit the compressibility reaches a minimum of $4.4 \times 10^{-5}\ P_a^{-1}$ around 45 °C before increasing again with increasing temperature. As the pressure is increased the compressibility decreases, being $3.9 \times 10^{-5}\ Pa^{-1}$ at 0 °C and 1000 bar. The bulk modulus of water is 2.2 GP_a. The low compressibility of non-gases, and of water in particular, leads to them often being assumed as incompressible. The low compressibility of water means that even in the deep oceans at 4000 m depth, where pressures are 4×107 Pa, there is only a 1.8% decrease in volume.

Triple Point

The temperature and pressure at which solid, liquid, and gaseous water coexist in equilibrium is called the triple point of water. This point is used to define the units of temperature (the kelvin, the SI unit of thermodynamic temperature and, indirectly, the degree Celsius and even the degree Fahrenheit). As a consequence, water's triple point temperature is a prescribed value rather than a measured quantity. The triple point is at a temperature of 273.16 K (0.01 °C) by convention, and at a pressure of 611.73 Pa. This pressure is quite low, about 1/166 of the normal sea level barometric pressure of 101,325 Pa. The atmospheric surface pressure on planet Mars is remarkably close to the triple point pressure, and the zero-elevation or "sea level" of Mars is defined by the height at which the atmospheric pressure corresponds to the triple point of water.

Although it is commonly named as "the triple point of water", the stable combination of liquid water, ice I, and water vapour is but one of several triple points on the phase diagram of water. Gustav Heinrich Johann Apollon Tammann in Göttingen produced data on several other triple points in the early 20th century. Kamb and others documented further triple points in the 1960s.

Surface Tension

Water drops are stable, due to the high surface tension of water, 72.8 mN/m, the highest of the nonmetallic liquids. This can be seen when small quantities of water are put on a surface such as glass: the water stays together as drops. This property is important for life. For example, when water is carried through xylem up stems in plants the strong intermolecular attractions hold the water column together. Strong cohesive properties hold the water column together, and strong adhesive properties stick the water to the xylem, and prevent tension rupture caused by transpiration pull. Other liquids with lower surface tension would have a higher tendency to "rip", forming vacuum or air pockets and rendering the xylem water transport inoperative.

ELECTRICAL PROPERTIES

Electrical Conductivity

Pure water containing no ions is an excellent insulator, but not even "deionized" water is completely free of ions.

Water undergoes auto-ionisation at any temperature above absolute zero. Further, because water is such a good solvent, it almost always has some solute dissolved in it, most frequently a salt. If water has even a tiny amount of such an impurity, then it can conduct electricity readily, as impurities such as salt separate into free ions in aqueous solution by which an electric current can flow.

It is known that the theoretical maximum electrical resistivity for water is approximately 182 kO·m^2/m (or 18.2 MO·cm^2/cm) at 25 °C. This figure agrees well with what is typically seen on reverse osmosis, ultrafilter and deionized ultrapure water systems used, for instance, in semiconductor manufacturing plants. A salt or acid contaminant level exceeding even 100 parts per trillion (ppt) in ultrapure water begins to noticeably lower its resistivity level by up to several kilohm-square meters per meter (a change of several hundred nanosiemens per meter of conductance).

Pure water has a low electrical conductivity, but this increases significantly upon solvation of a small amount of ionic material water such as hydrogen chloride. Thus the risks of electrocution are much greater in water with the usual impurities not found in pure water. (It is worth noting, however, that the risks of electrocution decrease when the impurities increase to the point where the water itself is a better conductor than the human body. For example, the risks of electrocution in sea water are lower than in fresh water, as the sea has a much higher level of impurities, particularly common salt, and the main current path will seek the better conductor. This is, nonetheless, not foolproof and substantial risks remain in salt water.) Any electrical properties observable in water are from the ions of mineral salts and carbon dioxide dissolved in it. Water does self-ionize where two water molecules become one hydroxide anion and one hydronium cation, but not enough to carry enough electric current to do any work or harm for most operations. In pure water, sensitive equipment can detect a very slight electrical conductivity of 0.055 μS/cm at 25 °C. Water can also be electrolyzed into oxygen and hydrogen gases but in the absence of dissolved ions this is a very slow process, as very little current is conducted. While electrons are the primary charge carriers in water (and metals), in ice (and some other electrolytes), protons are the primary carriers (see proton conductor).

Electrolysis

Water can be split into its constituent elements, hydrogen and oxygen, by passing an electric current through it. This process is called electrolysis. Water molecules naturally dissociate into H^+ and OH^- ions, which are pulled toward the cathode and anode, respectively. At the cathode, two H^+ ions pick up electrons and form H_2 gas. At the anode, four OH- ions combine and release O_2 gas, molecular water, and four electrons. The gases produced bubble to the surface, where they can be collected. The standard potential of the water electrolysis cell is 1.23 V at 25 °C.

Dipolar Nature of Water

An important feature of water is its polar nature. The water molecule forms an angle, with hydrogen atoms at the tips and oxygen at the vertex. Since oxygen has a higher electronegativity than hydrogen, the side of the molecule with the oxygen atom has a partial negative charge. A molecule with such a charge difference is called a dipole. The charge differences cause water molecules to be attracted to each other (the relatively positive areas being attracted to the relatively negative areas) and to other polar molecules. This attraction is known as hydrogen bonding, and explains many of the properties of water. Certain molecules, such as carbon dioxide, also have a difference in electronegativity between the atoms but the difference is that the shape of carbon dioxide is symmetrically aligned and so the opposing charges cancel one another out. This phenomenon of water can be seen if you hold an electrical source near a thin stream of water falling vertically, causing the stream to bend towards the electrical source.

Although hydrogen bonding is a relatively weak attraction compared to the covalent bonds within the water molecule itself, it is responsible for a number of water's physical properties. One such property is its relatively high melting and boiling point temperatures; more heat energy is required to break the hydrogen bonds between molecules. The similar compound hydrogen sulfide (H_2S), which has much weaker hydrogen bonding, is a gas at room temperature even though it has twice the molecular mass of water. The extra bonding between water molecules also gives liquid water a large specific heat capacity. This high heat capacity makes water a good heat storage medium.

Hydrogen bonding also gives water its unusual behavior when freezing. When cooled to near freezing point, the presence of hydrogen bonds means that the molecules, as they rearrange to minimize their energy, form the hexagonal crystal structure of ice that is actually of lower density: hence the solid form, ice, will float in water. In other words, water expands as it freezes, whereas almost all other materials shrink on solidification.

An interesting consequence of the solid having a lower density than the liquid is that ice will melt if sufficient pressure is applied. With increasing pressure the melting point temperature drops and when the melting point temperature is lower than the ambient temperature the ice begins to melt. A significant increase of pressure is required to lower the melting point temperature —the pressure exerted by an ice skater on the ice would only reduce the melting point by approximately 0.09 °C (0.16 °F).

Electronegative Polarity

Water has a partial negative charge (d^-) near the oxygen atom due to the unshared pairs of electrons, and partial positive charges (d^+) near the hydrogen atoms. In water, this happens because the oxygen atom is more electronegative than the hydrogen atoms—that is, it has a stronger "pulling power" on the molecule's electrons, drawing them closer (along with their negative charge) and making the area around the oxygen atom more negative than the area around both of the hydrogen atoms.

Adhesion

Water sticks to itself (cohesion) because it is polar. Water also has high adhesion properties because of its polar nature. On extremely clean/smooth glass the water may form a thin film because the molecular forces between glass and water molecules (adhesive forces) are stronger than the cohesive forces. In biological cells and organelles, water is in contact with membrane and protein surfaces that are hydrophilic; that is, surfaces that have a strong attraction to water. Irving Langmuir observed a strong repulsive force between hydrophilic surfaces. To dehydrate hydrophilic surfaces—to remove the strongly held layers of water of hydration—requires doing substantial work against these forces, called hydration forces. These forces are very large but decrease rapidly over a nanometer or less. Their importance in biology has been extensively studied by V. Adrian Parsegian of the National Institute of Health. They are particularly important when cells are dehydrated by exposure to dry atmospheres or to extracellular freezing.

Surface Tension

Water has a high surface tension caused by the strong cohesion between water molecules. This can be seen when small quantities of water are put onto a non-absorbent surface such as polythene and the water stays together as drops. Just as significantly, air trapped in surface disturbances forms bubbles, which sometimes last long enough to transfer gas molecules to the water. Another surface tension effect is capillary waves, which are the surface ripples that form around the impacts of drops on water surfaces, and sometimes occur with strong subsurface currents flowing to the water surface. The apparent elasticity caused by surface tension drives the waves.

Capillary Action

Capillary action refers to the process of water moving up a narrow tube against the force of gravity. It occurs because water adheres to the sides of the tube, and then surface tension tends to straighten the surface making the surface rise, and more water is pulled up through cohesion. The process is repeated as the water flows up the tube until there is enough water that gravity counteracts the adhesive force.

Water as a Solvent

Water is also a good solvent due to its polarity. Substances that will mix well and dissolve in water (e.g. salts) are known as "hydr s generate between other water molecules. If a substance has properties that do not allow it to overcome these strong intermolecular forces, the molecules are "pushed out" from the water, and do not dissolve. Contrary to the common misconception of a hydrophobic surface is energetically, but not entropically, favorable an ionic or polar compound enters water, it is surrounded by water molecules (Hydration). The relatively small size of water molecules typically allows many water molecules to surround one molecule of solute. The partially negative dipole ends of the water are attracted to positively charged components of the solute, and vice versa for the positive dipole ends.

In general, ionic and polar substances such as acids, alcohol, and salts are relatively soluble in water, and nonpolar substances such as fats and oils are not. Nonpolar molecules stay together in water because it is energetically more favorable for the water molecules to hydrogen bond to each other than to engage in van der Waals interactions with nonpolar molecules.

An example of an ionic solute is table salt; the sodium chloride, NaCl, separates into Na^+ cations and Cl^- anions, each being surrounded by water molecules. The ions are then easily transported away from their crystalline lattice into solution. An example of a nonionic solute is table sugar. The water dipoles make hydrogen bonds with the polar regions of the sugar molecule (OH groups) and allow it to be carried away into solution.

Water as a Ligand

The water molecule can also be used as a ligand in transition metal complexes; one example is perrhenic acid, which forms when Re_2O_7 is exposed to water. It contains two water molecules coordinated to a rhenium atom.

Amphoteric Nature of Water

Chemically, water is amphoteric — i.e., it is able to act as either an acid or a base. Occasionally the term hydroxide acid is used when water acts as an acid in a chemical reaction. At a pH of 7 (neutral), the concentration of hydroxide ions (OH^-) is equal to that of the hydronium (H_3O^+) or hydrogen (H^+) ions. If the equilibrium is disturbed, the solution becomes acidic (higher concentration of hydronium ions) or basic (higher concentration of hydroxide ions).

Water can act as either an acid or a base in reactions. According to the Brønsted-Lowry system, an acid is defined as a species which donates a proton (an H^+ ion) in a reaction, and a base as one which receives a proton. When reacting with a stronger acid, water acts as a base; when reacting with a stronger base, it acts as an acid. For instance, it receives an H+ ion from HCl in the equilibrium:

$$HCl + H_2O \rightleftharpoons H_3O^+ + Cl^-$$

Here water is acting as a base, by receiving an H^+ ion.

In the reaction with ammonia, NH_3, water donates an H^+ ion, and is thus acting as an acid:

$$NH_3 + H_2O \rightleftharpoons NH_4^+ + OH^-$$

Acidity in Nature

In theory, pure water has a pH of 7 at 298 K. In practice, pure water is very difficult to produce. Water left exposed to air for any length of time will rapidly dissolve carbon dioxide, forming a dilute solution of carbonic acid, with a limiting pH of about 5.7. As cloud droplets form in the atmosphere and as raindrops fall through the air minor amounts of CO_2 are absorbed and thus most rain is slightly acidic. If high amounts of nitrogen and sulfur oxides are present in the air, they too will dissolve into the cloud and rain drops producing more serious acid rain problems.

Hydrogen Bonding in Water

A water molecule can form a maximum of four hydrogen bonds because it can accept two and donate two hydrogens. Other molecules like hydrogen fluoride, ammonia, methanol form hydrogen bonds but they do not show anomalous behaviour of thermodynamic, kinetic or structural properties like those observed in water. The answer to the apparent difference between water and other hydrogen bonding liquids lies in the fact that apart from water none of the hydrogen bonding molecules can form four hydrogen bonds either due to an inability to donate/accept hydrogens or due to steric effects in bulky residues. In water local tetrahedral order due to the four hydrogen bonds gives rise to an open structure and a 3-dimensional bonding network, which exists in contrast to the closely packed structures of simple liquids. There is a great similarity between water and silica in their anomalous behaviour, even though one (water) is a liquid which has a hydrogen bonding network while the other (silica) has a covalent network with a very high melting point. One reason that water is well suited, and chosen, by life-forms, is that it exhibits its unique properties over a temperature regime that suits diverse biological processes, including hydration.

It is believed that hydrogen bond in water is largely due to electrostatic forces and some amount of covalency. The partial covalent nature of hydrogen bond predicted by Linus Pauling in the 1930s is yet to be proven unambiguously by experiments and theoretical calculations.

Quantum Properties of Molecular Water

Although the molecular formula of water is generally considered to be a stable result in molecular thermodynamics, recent work started in 1995 has shown that at certain scales, water may act more like $H_{3/2}O$ than H_2O at the quantum level. This result could have significant ramifications at the level of, for example, the hydrogen bond in biological, chemical and physical systems. The exp by a ratio of 1.5:1 of hydrogen to oxygen respectively. However, the time-scale of this response is only seen at the level of seconds (10-18 seconds), and so is only relevant in highly resolved kinetic and dynamical systems.

Heavy Water and isotopologues of water There are several isotopes of both hydrogen and oxygen, so several isotopologues of water are known. Hydrogen has three naturally occurring isotopes. The most common, making up more than 99.98% of the hydrogen in water, has 1 proton and 0 neutrons. A second isotope, deuterium (short form "D"), has 1 proton and 1 neutron. Deuterium oxide, D_2O, is also known as heavy water and is used in nuclear reactors as a neutron moderator. The third isotope, tritium, has 1 proton and 2 neutrons, and is radioactive, with a half-life of 4500 days. T_2O exists in nature only in tiny quantities, being produced primarily via cosmic ray-driven nuclear reactions in the atmosphere. D_2O is stable, but differs from H_2O in that it is denser - hence, "heavy water" - and in that several other physical properties are slightly different from those of common, Hydrogen-1 containing "light water". Water with one deuterium atom HDO occurs naturally in ordinary water in very low concentrations (~0.03%) and D_2O in far lower amounts (0.000003%). Consumption of pure isolated D_2O may affect biochemical processes - ingestion of large amounts impairs kidney and central nervous system function. However, very large amounts of heavy water must be consumed for any toxicity to be apparent, and smaller quantities can be consumed with no ill effects at all.

Transparency

Water's transparency is also an important property of the liquid. If water were not transparent, sunlight, essential to aquatic plants, would not reach into seas and oceans.

History

The properties of water have historically been used to define various temperature scales. Notably, the Kelvin, Celsius and Fahrenheit scales were, or currently are, defined by the freezing and boiling points of water. The less common scales of Delisle, Newton, Réaumur and Rømer were defined similarly. The triple point of water is a more commonly used standard point today.

Use

The first scientific decomposition of water into hydrogen and oxygen, by electrolysis, was done in 1800 by William Nicholson, an English chemist. In 1805, Joseph Louis Gay-Lussac and Alexander von Humboldt showed that water is composed of two parts hydrogen and one part oxygen (by volume).

Polywater was a hypothetical polymerized form of water that was the subject of much scientific controversy during the late 1960s. The consensus now is that it does not exist.

Systematic Naming

The accepted IUPAC name of water is simply "water" (or its equivalent in a different language), although there are two other systematic names which can be used to describe the molecule.

The simplest and best systematic name of water is hydrogen oxide. This is analogous to related compounds such as hydrogen peroxide, hydrogen sulfide, and deuterium oxide (heavy water). Another systematic name, oxidane, is accepted by IUPAC as a parent name for the systematic naming of oxygen-based substituent groups, although even these commonly have other recommended names. For example, the name hydroxyl is recommended over oxidanyl for the –OH group. The name oxane is explicitly mentioned by the IUPAC as being unsuitable for this purpose, since it is already the name of a cyclic ether also known as tetrahydropyran in the Hantzsch-Widman system; similar compounds include dioxane and trioxane.

Systematic Nomenclature

Dihydrogen monoxide or DHMO is an overly pedantic systematic covalent name of water. This term has been used in parodies of chemical research that call for this "lethal chemical" to be banned. In reality, a more realistic systematic name would be hydrogen oxide, since the "di-" and "mon-" prefixes are superfluous. Hydrogen sulfide, H_2S, is never referred to as "dihydrogen monosulfide", and hydrogen peroxide, H_2O_2, is never called "dihydrogen dioxide".

Other systematic names for water include hydroxic acid or hydroxylic acid. Likewise, the systematic alkali name of water is hydrogen hydroxide—both acid and alkali names exist for water because it is able to react both as an acid or an alkali, depending on the strength of the acid or alkali it is reacted with (it is amphoteric). None of these names are used widely outside of DHMO sites.

4 Hydrogen Bonding in Water

Hydrogen bonding occurs when an atom of hydrogen is attracted by rather strong forces to two atoms instead of only one, so that it may be considered to be acting as a bond between them. Typically hydrgen bonding occurs where the partially positively charged hydrogen atom lies between partially negatively charged oxygen and nitrogen atoms, but is also found elsewhere, such as between fluorine atoms in HF_2^- and between water and the smaller halide ions F^-, Cl^- and Br^-; the strength of hydrogen bonding reducing as the halide radius increases), and to a much smaller extent to I^- and even xenon Even very weak C-H····OH^2 hydrogen bonds (~ 4 kJ mol^{-1}) are being increasingly recognized. In theoretical studies, strong hydrogen bonds even occur to the hydrogen atoms in metal hydrides (for example, LiH···HF). The current view of the hydrogen bond has been reviewed. Hydrogen bonding is characterized by its preferred dimensions, molecular orientation, approximate linearity and changes in infrared frequency and intensity.

Water Hydrogen Bonds

In water's hydrogen bonds, the hydrogen atom is covalently attached to the oxygen of a water molecule (492.2148 kJ mol^{-1} but has (optimally) an additional attraction (about 23.3 kJ mol^{-1}a1 almost 5 x the average thermal collision fluctuation at 25°C)a2 to a neighbouring oxygen atom of another water molecule that is far greater than any included van der Waals interactioni. Hydrogen bonds within heavy water are stronger. Water's hydrogen bonding holds water molecules up to about 15% closer than if than if water was a simple liquid with just van der Waals interactions. However, as hydrogen bonding is directional it restricts the number of neighboring water molecules to about four rather than the larger number found in simple liquids (for example, xenon atoms have twelve nearest neighbours in the liquid state. Formation of hydrogen bonds between water molecules gives rise to large, but mostly compensating, energetic changes in enthalpy (becoming more negative) and entropy (becoming less positive). Both changes are particularly large, based by per-mass or per-volume basis, due to the small size of the water molecule. This enthalpy-entropy compensation is almost complete, however, with the consequence that very small imposed enthalpic or entropic effects may exert a considerable influence on aqueous systems. It is possible that hydrogen bonds between para-H_2O, possessing no ground state spin, are stronger and last longer than hydrogen bonds between orth-H_2O.

The hydrogen bond in water is part (about 90%) electrostatic and part (about 10%) covalent d and may be approximated by bonds made up of covalent HO-H····OH_2, ionic HOδ—Hδ+····Oδ-H_2, and long-bonded covalent HO^- ··H—O^+H_2 parts with HO-H····OH_2 being very much more in evidence than HO-··H—O+H_2, where there would be expected to be much extra non-bonded repulsion. Hydrogen bonding effects all the molecular orbitals even including the inner O1s (1a) orbital which is bound 318 kJ mol^{-1} (3.3 eV) less strongly in a tetrahedrally hydrogen bonded bulk liquid phase compared to the gas phase X-ray spectroscopic probing indicates that the electron transitions between molecular orbitals (changing with the local hydrogen bonding topology) with differing such contributions may shift on a time scale of less than a femtosecond. Contributing to the strength of water's hydrogen bonding are nuclear quantum effects (zero point vibrational energy) which bias the length of the O-H covalent bond longer than its 'equilibrium' position length (as the shorter HO-H····OH_2 hydrogen bonds are stronger), so also increasing the average dipole moment. On forming the hydrogen bond, the donor hydrogen atom stretches away from its oxygen atom and the acceptor lone-pair stretches away from its oxygen atom and towards the donor hydrogen atom, both oxygen atoms being pulled towards each other.

An important feature of the hydrogen bond is that it possesses direction; by convention this direction is that of the shorter O-H → covalent bond (the O-H hydrogen atom being donated to the O-atom acceptor atom on another H_2O molecule). In ^{1}H-NMR studies, the chemical shift of the proton involved in the hydrogen bond moves about 0.01 ppm K^{-1} upfield to lower frequency (plus about 5.5 ppm further upfield to vapor at 100°C); that is, becomes more shielded with reducing strength of hydrogen bonding as the temperature is raised; a similar effect may be seen in water's ^{17}O NMR, moving about 0.05 ppm K^{-1} upfield plus 36-38 ppm further upfield to vapor at 100°C. Increased extent of hydrogen bonding within clusters results in a similar effect; that is, higher NMR chemical shifts with greater cooperativity. The bond strength depends on its length and angle, with the strongest hydrogen bonding in water existing in the short linear proton-centered $H_5O_2^+$ ion at about 120 kJ mol^{-1}. However, small deviations from linearity in the bond angle (up to 20°) possibly have a relatively minor effect The dependency on bond length is very important and has been shown to exponentially decay with distance. Some researchers consider the hydrogen bond to be brokenc if the bond length is greater than 3.10 Å or the bond angle less than 146° 2 although ab initio calculations indicate that most of the bonding energy still remains and more bent but shorter bonds may be relatively strong; for example, one of the hydrogen bonds in ice-four (143°). Similarly O····H-O interaction energies below 10 kJ mol^{-1} have been taken as indicative of broken hydrogen bonds although they are almost 50% as strong as 'perfect' hydrogen bonds and there is no reason to presuppose that it is solely the hydrogen bond that has been affected with no contributions from other interactions. Also, the strength of bonding must depend on the orientation and positions of the other bonded and non-bonded atoms and 'lone pair' electrons There is a trade-off between the covalent and hydrogen bond strengths; the stronger is the H····O bond, the weaker the O-H covalent bond, and the shorter the O····O distance. The weakening of the O-H covalent bond gives rise to a good indicator of hydrogen bonding energy; the fractional increase in its length determined by the increasing strength of the hydrogen bonding for example, when the pressure is substantially increased (~ GPa) the remaining hydrogen bonds (H····O) are forced shorter causing the O-H covalent bonds to be elongated. Hydrogen bond strength can be affected by electromagnetic and magnetic effects. Dissociation is a rare event, occurring only twice a day that is, only once for every 10^{16} times the hydrogen bond breaks.

The anomalous properties of liquid water may be explained primarily on the basis of its hydrogen bonding.

Hydrogen Bond Cooperativity

When a hydrogen bond forms between two water molecules, the redistribution of electrons changes the ability for further hydrogen bonding. The water molecule donating the hydrogen atom has increased electron density in its 'lone pair' region which encourages hydrogen bond acceptance, and the accepting water molecule has reduced electron density centered on its hydrogen atoms and its remaining 'lone pair' region which encourages further donation but discourages further acceptance of hydrogen bonds. This electron redistribution thus results in both the cooperativity (e.g. accepting one hydrogen bond encourages the donation of another) and anticooperativity (for example, accepting one hydrogen bond discourages acceptance of another) in hydrogen bond formation in water networks. Cooperative hydrogen bonding increases the O-H bond length whilst causing a 20-fold greater reduction in the H····O and O····O distances . The increase in bond length has been correlated with the hydrogen bond strength and resultant O-H stretch vibrations Thus O····O distances within clusters are likely to be shorter than those at the periphery, in agreement with the icosahedral cluster model. If the hydrogen bond is substantially bent then it follows that the bond strength is weaker. The main criteria to determine the strength of hydrogen bonds are their (relatively inaccurately determined) intermolecular distances and the (more precise) wavenumbers of their stretching vibrational modes and those of the donor hydrogen covalent bond.e Any factors, such as polarization, that reduces the hydrogen bond length, is expected to increase its covalency. There is still some dispute over the size of this covalency,d however any covalency will increase the network stability relative to purely electrostatic effects. The hydrogen bond in water dimers is sufficiently strong to result in the dimers persisting within the gas state at significant concentrations (for example, ~0.1% H_2O at 25°C and 85% humidity) to contribute significantly to the absorption of sunlight and atmospheric reaction kinetics . The molecular orbitals involved in the hydrogen bonding between two water molecules (50 KB) and five water molecules (29 KB) in a cyclic pentamer.

Although the hydrogen atoms are often shown along lines connecting the oxygen atoms, this is now thought to be indicative of time-averaged direction only and unlikely to be found to a significant extent even in ice.

Liquid water consists of a mixture of short, straight and strong hydrogen bonds and long, weak and bent hydrogen bonds with many intermediate between these extremes. Short hydrogen bonds in water are strongly correlated with them being straighter . Proton magnetic shielding studies give the following average parameters for the instantaneous structure of liquid water at 4°C; non-linearity, distances and variance; all increasing with temperature.

Note that the two water molecules below are not restricted to perpendicular planes and only a small proportion of hydrogen bonds are likely to have this averaged structure.

The hydrogen bond length of water varies with temperature and pressure. As the covalent bond lengths vary much less with temperature and pressure, most of the densification of ice Ih due to reduced temperature or increased pressure must be due to reduction in the hydrogen bond length. This hydrogen bond length variation can be shown from the changes in volume of ice Ih . As hydrogen bond strength depends almost linearly on its length (shorter length giving stronger hydrogen bonding), it also depends almost linearly (outside extreme values) on the temperature and pressure.

The latest molecular parameters for water are given elsewhere. At 0 K the O····O distance in ice Ih is 2.75 Å. The energy of a linear hydrogen bond depends on the orientation of the water molecules relative to the hydrogen bond.

Note that in liquid water, the instantaneous hydrogen bonded arrangement of most molecules is not as symmetrical as shown here. In particular, the positioning of the water molecules donating hydrogen bonds to the accepting positions on a water molecule are likely to be less tetrahedrally placed, due to the lack of substantial tetrahedrally positioned 'lone pair' electrons, than those water molecules that are being donated to from that water molecule. Also, the arrangement may well consist of one pair of more tetrahedrally arranged strong hydrogen bonds (one donor and one acceptor) with the remaining hydrogen bond pair (one donor and one acceptor) being either about 6 kJ mol-1 weaker, less tetrahedrally arranged or bifurcated perhaps mainly due to the anticooperativity effects mentioned below. Such a division of water into higher (4-linked) and lower (2-linked) hydrogen bond coordinated water has been shown by modeling X-ray absorption spectroscopy confirms that, at room temperature, 80% of the molecules of liquid water have one (cooperatively strengthened) strong hydrogen bonded O-H group and one non-, or only weakly, bonded O-H group at any instant (sub-femtosecond averaged and such as may occur in pentagonally hydrogen bonded clusters), the remaining 20% of the molecules being made up of four-hydrogen-bonded tetrahedrally coordinated clusters There is much debate as to whether such structuring represents the more time-averaged structure, which is understood by some to be basically tetrahedral.

Liquid water contains by far the densest hydrogen bonding of any solvent with almost as many hydrogen bonds as there are covalent bonds. These hydrogen bonds can rapidly rearrange in response to changing conditions and environments (for example, solutes). The hydrogen bonding patterns are random in water (and ice Ih); for any water molecule chosen at random, there is equal probability (50%) that the four hydrogen bonds (that is, the two hydrogen donors and the two hydrogen acceptors) are located at any of the four sites around the oxygen. Water molecules surrounded by four hydrogen bonds tend to clump together, forming clusters, for both statistical and energetic reasons.

Hydrogen bonded chains (that is, O-H····O-H····O) are cooperative the breakage of the first bond is the hardest, then the next one is weakened, and so on (see the cyclic water pentamer). Thus unzipping may occur with complex macromolecules held together by hydrogen bonding, for example, nucleic acids. Such cooperativity is a fundamental property of liquid water where hydrogen bonds are up to 250% stronger than the single hydrogen bond in the dimer. A strong base at the end of a chain may strengthen the bonding further. The cooperative nature of the hydrogen bond means that acting as an acceptor strengthens the water molecule acting as a donor. However, there is an anticooperative aspect in so far as acting as a donor weakens the capability to act as another donor, for example, O····H-O-H····O It is clear therefore that a water molecule with two hydrogen bonds where it acts as both donor and acceptor is somewhat stabilized relative to one where it is either the donor or acceptor of two. This is the reason why it is suspected that the first two hydrogen bonds (donor and acceptor) give rise to the strongest hydrogen bonds . An interesting way of describing the cooperative/anticooperative nature of the water dimer hydrogen bond is to use the nomenclature d'a'DAd''a'' where DA represents the donor-acceptor nature of the hydrogen bond, the d'a' represents the remaining donor-acceptor status of the donating water molecule and d''a'' represents the remaining donor-acceptor status of the accepting water molecule Individually, the most energetically favored donating water molecules have the structures 02D, 12D, 01D and 11D with 00D and 10D disfavored whereas the most energetically favored accepting water molecules have the structures A20, A21, A10 and A11 with A00 and A01 disfavoured.

Cations may induce strong cooperative hydrogen-bonding around them due to the polarization of water O-H by cation-lone pair interactions (Cation+····O-H····O-H). A cooperativity factor for this effect, which varied as the

Hofmeister series from K^+ was introduced (1.08) to Zn^{2+} (2.5). Total hydrogen bonding around ions may be disrupted however as if the electron pair acceptance increases (for example, in water around cations) so the electron pair donating power of these water molecules is reduced; with opposite effects in the hydration water around anions. These changes in the relative hydration ability of salt solutions are responsible for the swelling and deswelling behavior of hydrophilic polymer gels.

The substantial cooperative strengthening of hydrogen bond in water is dependent on long range interactions Breaking one bond generally weakensf those around whereas making one bond generally strengthens those around and this, therefore, encourages larger clusters, for the same average bond density. The hydrogen-bonded cluster size in water at 0°C has been estimated to be 400 . Weakly hydrogen-bonding surface restricts the hydrogen-bonding potential of adjacent water so that these make fewer and weaker hydrogen bonds. As hydrogen bonds strengthen each other in a cooperative manner, such weak bonding also persists over several layers and may cause locally changed solvation. Conversely, strong hydrogen bonding will be evident at distance. The weakening of hydrogen bonds, from about 23 kJ mol-1 to about 17 kJ mol-1, is observed when many bonds are broken at superheating temperatures (> 100°C) so reducing the cooperativity The breakage of these bonds is not only due to the more energetic conditions at high temperature but also results from a related reduction in the hydrogen bond donating ability by about 10% for each 100°C increase The loss of these hydrogen bonds results in a small increase in the hydrogen bond accepting ability of water, due possibly to increased accessibility.

Every hydrogen bond formed increases the hydrogen bond status of two water molecules and every hydrogen bond broken reduces the hydrogen bond status of two water molecules. The network is essentially complete at ambient temperatures; that is, (almost) all molecules are linked by at least one unbroken hydrogen bonded pathway. Hydrogen bond lifetimes are 1-20 ps whereas broken bond lifetimes are about 0.1 ps with the proportion of 'dangling' hydrogen bonds persisting for longer than a picosecond being insignificant Broken bonds are basically unstable and will probably reform to give same hydrogen bond (as shown by the slow ortho-water/para-water equilibrium process particularly if the other three hydrogen bonds are in place; hydrogen bond breakage being more dependent on the local structuring rather than the instantaneous hydrogen bond strength If not, breakage usually leads to rotation around one of the remaining hydrogen bond(s) and not to translation away, as the resultant 'free' hydroxyl group and 'lone pair' are both quite reactive. Also important, if seldom recognized, is the possibility of the hydrogen bond breaking, as evidenced by physical techniques such as IR, Raman or NMR and caused by loss of hydrogen bond 'covalency' due to electron rearrangement, without any angular change in the O-H····O atomic positions. Thus, clusters may persist for much longer times than common interpretation of data from these methods indicates. Evidence for this may be drawn from the high degree of hydrogen bond breakage seen in the IR spectrum of ice where the clustering is taken as lasting essentially forever.

Rearranging Hydrogen Bonds

Water's hydrogen bonds only reorient when there is an available partner able to accept the bond, with the strength of the broken hydrogen bond playing little or no role The molecular orbitals of water indicate that the two 'lone pairs' of electrons do not give distinct directed electron density in isolated molecules, with tetrahedral nature of water's hydrogen bonding due to four-coordination involving two donor and two acceptor hydrogen bonds. However trigonal (approximately planar) hydrogen bonding is also possible with two donor and one acceptor hydrogen bonds associated with individual water molecules. The lack of substantial tetrahedrally positioned 'lone pair' electrons may ease this process, at a cost of one hydrogen bond energy. Also the acceptor hydrogen bond in three coordinated but tetrahedral arrangements (two donor and one acceptor hydrogen bonds with one vacant acceptor site) can slide through a planar arrangement to the vacant tetrahedral site without breaking. This flexibility in the hydrogen bonding topology facilitates hydrogen-bonding rearrangements.

Bifurcated Hydrogen Bonds

Bifurcated hydrogen bonds (where both hydrogen atoms from one water molecule are hydrogen bonding to the same other water molecule, or one hydrogen atom simultaneously forms hydrogen bonds to two other water molecules) have just under half the strength of a normal hydrogen bond (per half the bifurcated bond) and present a low-energy route for hydrogen-bonding rearrangements They allow the constant randomization of the hydrogen bonding within the network. However, it should be noted that they require the breakage of two hydrogen bonds; one hydrogen bond to form the bifurcated arrangement and another to make way for a different hydrogen bond to form. Any necessary rotation may also involve bending or stretching other hydrogen bonds. Bifurcation of hydrogen bonds cannot cause their net breakage and only occur when a broken hydrogen bond releases a lone pair to accept the incoming hydrogen bond donor Trifurcated hydrogen bonds (where one hydrogen atom simultaneously forms hydrogen bonds to three other water molecules, forming a tetrahedral face) may also form but only have about one sixth the strength of a normal hydrogen bond per third of the bifurcated bond require free lone pairs on all three bound water molecules and the rest of local cluster must also be poorly hydrogen bonded.

Information Transfer

Hydrogen bonding carries information about solutes and surfaces over significant distances in liquid water. The effect is synergistic, directive and extensive. Thus, in the diagram opposite, strong hydrogen-bonding in molecule (1), caused by solutes or surfaces, will be transmitted to molecules 2 and 3, then to 5 and 6 and then as combined power to 8.

The effect is reinforced by additional polarization effects and the resonant intermolecular transfer of O-H vibrational energy, mediated by dipole-dipole interactions and the hydrogen bonds Reorientation of one molecule induces corresponding motions in the neighbours.

Thus solute molecules can 'sense' (for example, effect each others solubility) each other at distances of several nanometers and surfaces may have effects extending to tens of nanometers. This long range correlation of molecular orientation has recently been confirmed using hyper-Rayleigh light scattering and is a reason for the high dielectric constant of water and the consequential reduction in this dielectric constant as the temperature is raised and the number of hydrogen bonds is reduced Where water molecules are next to flat hydrophobic surfaces, and unable to form extensive clathrate structuring, some hydrogen bonds must be broken and the water molecules will tend to change orientation, from one hydrogen bond directed orthogonally away from the surface (as in clathrates) to one hydrogen bond directed orthogonally towards the surface, in order to minimize the energy requirement. Also the water molecules tend to collapse into their shallow energy minima due to increased non-bonded interactions. Although there may be a consequentially increased density in the first water layer, the second and subsequent water shells compensate by forming stronger hydrogen bonds and a less dense structure. Consequences of this include differential solvation properties affecting surface absorption.

Hydrogen bonding rearrangement offers a low energy pathway for the transfer of hydrogen atoms during tautomerism, in a way similar to Grotthuss mechanism for hydrogen ion transport. Shown opposite is adenine tautomerism that can give rise to Adenine - Cytosine (mutation producing) pairing, which uses the rare tautomer on the left.

5 Fresh Water Natural Composition

Although water has the simple formula H2O, it is a complex chemical solution. "Pure" water essentially is nonexistent in the natural environment. Natural water, whether in the atmosphere, on the ground surface, or under the ground, always contains dissolved minerals and gases as a result of its interaction with the atmosphere, minerals in rocks, organic matter, and living organisms.

Chemical Controls of Water Composition

The acidity of water is gauged by its pH, which is a measure of the concentration of the hydrogen ion (H^+) in the solution according to the relationship pH = -log(H^+). The higher the concentration of H^+ in the water, the lower its pH, and the greater its acidity. Acid waters have a pH less than 7 (neutral pH is 7), with the most acid waters at pH 1 or less. Basic (alkaline) waters have a pH greater than 7, with the most basic waters at pH 14.

Natural Acidity

Natural rainwater is slightly acidic because it interacts with carbon dioxide (CO_2) in the atmosphere, forming carbonic acid (H_2CO_3). Some of the carbonic acid in the rainwater then breaks down (dissociates), producing more hydrogen ion and bicarbonate ion, both of which are dissolved in the rainwater.

The two reactions in rainwater are as follows:

$$H_2O + CO_2 = H_2CO_3 \quad (5.1)$$

$$H_2CO_3 = HCO_3^- + H^+ \quad (5.2)$$

The hydrogen ion produced by the second reaction lowers the pH of rain-water. How far it lowers it from the neutral value of 7 depends on how much carbonic acid is in the water as a result of the first reaction, although a limit exists as defined by the *equilibrium constant* of the reaction. The concentration of carbonic acid, then, depends on how much carbon dioxide is in the atmosphere. In other words, when more CO_2 is present, more acid is produced, and the water becomes more acidic.

The Earth's atmosphere presently contains, on average, approximately 0.3 per cent carbon dioxide. Using this value in the two reactions above, hydrologists can calculate that the concentration of H^+ in rainwater at chemical equilibrium is $10^{-5.7}$ moles per liter. This concentration is equivalent to a pH of 5.7, a calculated figure that is close to many actual measurements of rainwater. Because pH 7 is neutral, pH 5.7 is considered slightly acidic. Although natural rain is slightly acidic owing to the natural reaction between rainwater and atmospheric carbon dioxide, the term "acid rain" usually is applied to rainwater that has been made unnaturally acidic by human-caused emissions of nitrogen and sulfur oxides.

Dissolution

Slightly acidic rainwater reacts with land-derived dust particles in the atmosphere. These reactions result in the rainwater gaining dissolved calcium (Ca^{2+}), magnesium (Mg^{2+}), sodium (Na^+), potassium (K^+), and other elements.

Although carbonic acid is a weak acid, it is very effective over geologic time. Carbonic acid is largely responsible for the breakdown of rocks to soil during chemical weathering and the formation of limestone caverns and sinkholes. The lower the pH, the more acidic the water, and the more minerals it can dissolve.

Sea spray, carried aloft by winds blowing across the ocean, contributes to dissolved constituents in rainwater. Although dissolved minerals from spray are more abundant in coastal areas, they occur through out the atmosphere. Sea spray is the primary source of chloride (Cl^-) in rainwater and a significant amount of sodium (Na^+).

Oxidizing–Reducing Reactions

Oxidizing–reducing reactions change the charge of an ion as it gains or loses an electron. The solubility of some elements in water depends on whether they are oxidized or reduced. The natural environment may control in which state the element occurs. In the natural environment, iron (Fe) can exist either as reduced iron (Fe^{2+}) or oxidized iron (Fe^{3+}).

Iron is more soluble in the reduced state than it is in the oxidized state, where it often occurs as an iron oxide mineral (Fe_2O_3). Therefore, if the local environment produces the reduced iron form, the water will have higher concentrations of dissolved iron.

The most common causes of a reducing environment are oxidation reactions involving organic matter. The oxidation of an organic molecule can result in iron, existing as a solid iron oxide mineral (Fe_2O_3), being dissolved into the water as reduced iron (Fe_2^+). Other elements that behave similarly include manganese (Mn), sulfur (S) and nitrogen (N).

Streams and Lakes

The composition of stream and lake water varies from one place to another, and within a single watershed varies both seasonally and along the stream's path. The major source of dissolved minerals in streams and lakes is the rocks the water moves over and through along its path from where it falls as precipitation to where it exits the watershed or enters the lake. As the slightly acidic water encounters rocks, the minerals begin to dissolve and contribute their elements to the water. The type of rocks in the watershed influence stream-water composition. A stream flowing over sedimentary rocks will have a different composition than a stream flowing over *igneous* rocks.

Also contributing to stream-water and lake-water composition are reactions between the water and the biomass, particularly in forests. Leaves and branches help neutralize the pH of the precipitation and contribute dissolved elements. Biologic activity in the stream or lake (e.g., photosynthesis) can change pH and dissolved oxygen content. Temperature influences the amount of dissolved gases (e.g., oxygen).

Stream-water composition changes from headwaters to outlet because the water is in contact with the rocks and sediments of the streambed for cumulatively longer times. Also, tributaries draining different geologic areas may enter the stream, and groundwater may seep into the stream. In pools or other slow-moving stream segments, oxidizing and reducing reactions may occur where organic matter accumulates.

Seasonal variations in stream-water composition may reflect differing precipitation amounts, as well as the portion of the stream's flow that is contributed by groundwater. In the drier times of the year the proportion of groundwater contribution is greater than in the wet season.

Lake-water composition is influenced by evaporation, among many other factors. As water evaporates, the dissolved minerals are left behind. The more evaporation, the higher the concentration of dissolved minerals (salts) in the water. If evaporation continues far enough, minerals such as calcite ($CaCO_3$) or gypsum ($CaSO_4 \cdot 2H_2O$) may precipitate from the solution. The Great Salt Lake in Utah began as a freshwater lake (Lake Bonneville) during the last Ice Age. Progressive evaporation as the climate became arid has made it saltier than the ocean (see Table 5.1).

Groundwater

Many of the factors that influence the surface water composition also influence groundwater composition. Groundwater is always in contact with rocks and minerals and moves more slowly than surface water—centimeters per day instead of kilometers per hour. As a result, groundwater often contains more dissolved minerals than surface water.

When water seeps below the surface, it passes through the soil where microbial *respiration* processes release CO_2. As water encounters the CO_2, the pH is lowered, and the water can dissolve more minerals. At higher temperatures, minerals dissolve more readily. Deep groundwater tends to be warmer (e.g., the source of water from hot springs) and, as a result, has higher mineral content.

Ultimately, what controls the composition of groundwater is:

1. the geologic materials groundwater is moving through;
2. the type of reactions taking place; and
3. the contact time, or length of time groundwater has been in contact with the rocks.

The contact time may vary from a few days to more than 10,000 years. The table shows analyses of groundwater from different geologic formations [analyses (1) and (10) of Table 5.1] and differing contact times [analyses (11) and (12) of Table 5.1].

Knowledge of water–rock–organism reactions helps hydrologists unravel the origin of a specific water parcel. Carefully analyzing the water allows them to identify what types of reactions have affected the water, and to understand the geological and ecological history of the area.

Table 5.1: Example composition of precipitation

	(1)	(2)	(3)	(4)	(5)	(6)	(7)	(8)	(9)	(10)	(11)	(12)
Calcium	0.8	0.65	40.7	1.68	14	22	241	400	144	6.5	3.11	4540
Magnesium	1.2	0.14	7.2	0.24	13	17	7200	1350	55	1.1	0.7	160
Sodium	9.4	0.56	1.4	0.16	8	14	83600	10500	~27	~37	3.03	2740
Potassium	–	0.11	1.2	0.31	–	0.5	4070	380	~2	~3	1.09	32.1
Bicarbonate	4	–	114	5.4	104	129	251	28	622	77	20	55
Sulfate	7.6	2.2	36	1.3	4.7	1.3	16400	185	60	15	1.0	1
Chloride	17	0.57	1.1	0.06	8.5	33	140000	19000	53	17	0.5	12600

(Contd...)

	(1)	(2)	(3)	(4)	(5)	(6)	(7)	(8)	(9)	(10)	(11)	(12)
Silica	0.3	–	3.7	0.7	24	30	48	3	22	103	16.4	8.5
TDS	38	4.7	207	10	120	180	254000	35000	670	222	36	20338
pH	5.5	–	–	6.9	7.7	7.0	7.4	–	–	6.7	6.2	6.5

Note: All concentrations in milligrams/liter. TDS is total dissolved solids and pH is a measure of the acidity of the water. A pH less than 7 is acidic. A dash (-) indicates that the component was not detected or the water was not analyzed for this constituent. A tilde (~) means "approximately."

Key to Analyses:

1. Rainwater from Menlo Park, California;
2. Average rainwater from sites in North Carolina and Virginia;
3. Composition of the Rhine River as it leaves the Alps;
4. Stream draining igneous rocks in the Washington Cascades;
5. Jump-Off Joe Creek, southwestern Oregon, wet season, November, 1990;
6. Jump-Off Joe Creek, southwestern Oregon, dry season, September, 1991;
7. Great Salt Lake, Utah;
8. Average seawater;
9. Groundwater from limestone of the Supai Formation, Grand Canyon;
10. Groundwater from volcanic rocks, New Mexico;
11. Groundwater from a spring, Sierra Nevada Mountains: short residence time; and
12. Groundwater from metamorphic rocks in Canada: long residence time.

Origin of Saline Groundwater

Typically, groundwater has a total dissolved solids (TDS) content of less than 250 milligrams/liter (mg/L). In some areas, however, groundwater with a TDS of greater than 100,000 mg/L is found. (Sea water has a TDS content of approximately 35,000 mg/L.) Saline groundwater has been found in a variety of geologic environments, commonly in marine sedimentary rocks, but also in ancient metamorphic and igneous rocks.

Saline groundwater can form in at least three ways i.e., (1) from trapped sea water; (2) from dissolving highly soluble minerals; and (3) as a result of a long contact time with rocks, and thus chemical reaction time with surrounding rocks.

- *Trapped Sea Water (connate water).* When marine sediments are deposited, some sea water commonly remains trapped between the mineral grains. Connate water later may migrate through the rocks as groundwater.
- *Highly Soluble Minerals.* Groundwater encountering easily dissolved minerals such as gypsum ($CaSO_4 2H_2O$) or halite (NaCl), will become saltier.
- *Contact Time.* Groundwater that follows deep paths below the ground may be in contact and able to react with rocks for thousands or tens of thousands of years. This groundwater will acquire a higher TDS with time.

The Nature of Ice

Ice is an allotrope of water substance, a crystalline solid stable below 0 °C, though it sublimes slowly to water vapor at low water vapor pressures. Ice, water and vapor coexist at the triple point at T = 0.01 °C and p = 4.579 mmHg. If the temperature and pressure vary from these values, one of the three phases disappears, and the other two reach an equilibrium. Ice and air-saturated water are in equilibrium at 0 °C or 273.15K, an important reference point for thermometry. Although ice melts at 0 °C, water must be cooled below this temperature to initiate ice formation, after which the mixture warms and freezes as rapidly as heat can be removed. This is called supercooling.

Ice can be used in freezing mixtures to produce temperatures well below the normal melting point of ice. This, and the use of antifreezes, is treated in Phase Rule, since some thermodynamics of mixtures is needed to treat it properly. Salt is the normal substance added for this purpose, as in the traditional making of ice cream.

Ice is a mineral (a naturally-occurring substance of constant chemical composition) and Dana regards it as such, although many mineralogy books do not. It is permanent in polar regions where the average temperature is below 0 °C, and of temporary occurrence elsewhere. The greatest accumulations are in the large ice sheets of Greenland and Antarctica. Other permanent accumulations are found in mountain glaciers and snowfields. The flow of glaciers is the best evidence of the flow of matter considered as a solid when long times are involved. The passage of a weighted piano wire through a block of ice without cutting the ice into two pieces is another example of the same thing, often erroneously explained as melting followed by freezing ("regelation").

Pure ice is clear and transparent. In large thicknesses, transmitted light appears blue because of the tail of an infrared absorption due to the protons (hydrogen nuclei) in it. This is not the blue of the sky, Rayleigh-scattering blue, but a greenish absorption blue. Ice is soft, 1.5 on Moh's scale, between talc and gypsum, so cutting it will not dull knives. Ice can easily be scratched by the fingernail. It is brittle, breaking with a conchoidal fracture, and has no cleavage. Its density at 0 °C is 0.91671 g/cc, less than that of water, which has many important consequences. Among these are the fact that icebergs float and do not sink to the bottom of the ocean, which was disastrous to the RMS Titanic in 1912. If icebergs were pure ice (which they are not), they would float with a fraction 0.92 submerged and 0.08 visible. Some Antarctic icebergs have an average density of only 0.83, so they float with 0.17 visible. Icebergs usually contain entangled air and rock débris. The surface ice formed on natural water bodies in the winter remains on the surface, hindering the freezing of the water below it by its low thermal conductivity. Life can survive through the winter in the cold water in all but the smallest ponds. The sea itself benefits from this; there is always water beneath the Arctic ice. Water has maximum density at about 4 °C, so it is already expanding as it approaches freezing. In lakes, water cooler than this descends and is replaced by warmer water from below, which in turn is cooled. Only when the whole body is at 4° does freezing begin at the surface. Dense 4° water makes an isothermal layer in a lake. The water above this increases rapidly in temperature as the warmer surface is approached, forming a region called the thermocline.

The expansion on freezing also has another wide-ranging effect. Water is attracted by capillary action into fine cracks in rocks and road pavements. When it freezes, the crack is powerfully wedged wider. This makes ice the most powerful weathering agent in geology, in an almost unseen process whose results are soon evident. Water is a powerful agent of chemical weathering, which takes advantage of the mechanical action of the ice. Between them, they create the surface of the planet that we see.

Stones embedded in finer material are forced upwards by alternate freezing and thawing, an example of a general phenomenon called frost heaving. This can produce remarkable structures, such as the gravel circles of Spitzbergen. These are rings of coarse stones about 1 m in diameter that are almost perfect circles, and whose origin has long been a mystery. Recent computer simulations have suggested how these circles can be produced by frost heaving. Stones apparently come to the surface both in regions where the earth is not permanently frozen, and in permafrost areas. Of course, in either case the surface must not be permanently frozen, but in one case the freezing is a surface phenomenon, and in the other it is the melting. At depth, the earth will always be at a constant temperature.

A possible mechanism by which stones are sorted and pushed to the surface is illustrated in the figure. At depth, we presume the earth is at a constant temperature of +5°. The 0° isotherm rises and falls with the surface temperature. When it reaches the surface, the earth is thawed. In arctic permafrost areas, the behavior may be the opposite, with the earth permanently frozen below, and the surface alternately frozen and thawed. On the left, the 0° isotherm is falling, and the stone is plucked upwards since it freezes in at the top, allowing thawed material to come in beneath. On the right, the 0° isotherm is rising. The stone is held up by being frozen in at the top, while the earth around the lower part contracts. This mechanism obviously fails if conditions are reversed, and the earth at depth is constantly frozen, not thawed. The heaving occurs when the 0° isotherm is moving by the stone, and must result in relative motion between the stone and its matrix. It would be good to have a clear explanation of the mechanism, but I have not seen one so far. In making gravel circles, the depression of the 0° isotherm causes the frost heaving to make piles of stones by a feedback effect. The Physics Today article in the References has pictures and further information.

Ice is slippery, with a low coefficient of friction, even with dry, and this is accentuated when the surface is lubricated with water. At 0 °C, the static coefficient of friction of ice on ice is 0.05-0.15, while the kinetic coefficient is about 0.02. These numbers increase at lower temperatures, about doubling at -12 °C. Brass on ice gives 0.02 at 0 °C, and

0.085 at -20 °C. Waxed hickory (skis) give 0.09 at 0.1 m/s, and 0.03 at 4.0 m/s. We can conclude that the coefficient of friction decreases with speed and increases with lowered temperature. A coefficient of friction of 0.02 means that sliding will begin (static) or proceed at constant speed (dynamic) on a 1:50 gradient. It is often said that the pressure under the blade of an ice skate melts some ice and lubricates the motion, but the pressure and the magnitude of the effect are insufficient for this to be valid. It is simply that the ice is slippery anyway, especially not far from the melting point. Runners are very satisfactory as a substitute for wheels, especially when wheels would sink into the snow, and their use is traditional in cold climates.

When ice freezes from water, dissolved gases and other substances in the water, such as salt, are rejected and the ice is pure water (practically, of course, there are usually inclusions of the impurities in the ice, but they are not part of the crystal). This is easily seen in ordinary ice cubes, where the last part to freeze in the centre is usually cloudy with these inclusions. If distilled water is boiled and then frozen, the ice will be clear, as can be verified in your kitchen. Sea-water could, in principle, be desalinated by freezing, but the cost of the energy to refrigerate the water is prohibitive, unless natural cold is used. Separating the impurities is also a difficult matter.

Water vapour forms ice crystals in the atmosphere, which then fall as precipitation. This is quite pure water, since it has been purified by evaporation. It is easier for rain to form by the melting of falling ice crystals than by the direct formation of water droplets, which requires a high degree of supersaturation. Snow is formed from hexagonal, dendritic single crystals of remarkable beauty. Although the substance of the snow is clear and transparent, it appears pure white when it falls because of the scattering of the light from the very irregular surface. A similar effect occurs in white paint: titanium dioxide, a white pigment, is actually clear and transparent, but when finely ground appears white. A substance that is not transparent appears black under the same circumstances. White and black are subjective color perceptions; they have no consistent physical meaning.

The main kinds of ice crystals that form in the atmosphere are columns, plates and needles. The beautiful snowflakes with hexagonal symmetry, or stellar crystals, are actually rather rare. It is often said that no two snowflakes are alike, because of the seemingly infinite variety in them, but many snowflakes are really quite similar. Snow rarely consists of perfect crystals, but more often as fragments and clumps and balls of dendritic pieces, with an occasional more perfect plate or star. Columns form at the lowest temperatures, around -40 °C, plates and stars at intermediate temperatures, and needles at the lower temperatures, from -8 °C to 0 °C. Columns falling through lower regions may become capped with plates on one or both ends. The columns formed in high cirrostratus are the ones responsible for the 22° halo. The hexagonal columns and plates adopt a particular attitude when falling because of their aerodynamics. Such bodies turn to an orientation of highest drag, which for plates is horizontal, and for columns sideways. Refraction of the light of the sun or moon by such oriented crystals cause the attractive halo phenomena that will be discussed below.

Many curiosities are associated with snowfall. The wind can blow small lumps of snow that pick up more snow as they roll along, becoming large snow rollers of striking appearance. Icicles grow and melt; hydromites are analogous to stalagmites. Ice freezes on wires and spiderwebs from supercooled moist air. Noise can come from snowbanks, as it comes from sand dunes. Indeed, snow can make drifts analogous to sand dunes, of which the sastrugi (apparently singular) is an example, having special textures of snow. Blowing snow, already fallen, in winds faster than 35 mph is a blizzard. Frost grows in dendritic patterns on windowpanes. Rime is a poetic name for hoarfrost, white frost, caused as explained above ("hoar" is a word for grey). Rime in meteorology always means ice consisting of crystals fused together. Glaze ice is the same, but clear and transparent, or glassy. These two kinds of ice are distinguished in aircraft icing, where they have different effects.

Cold streams in which the water is near freezing can also create ice beneath the surface. Frazil is a spongy ice formed when very cold surface water mixes with lower water and freezes. It can be carried along with the stream and collect where its progress is hindered. Rocks and other bodies beneath the surface may be cooled below 0 °C by radiation in quieter waters, and a surface layer of ice may form on them. Supercooled water will also freeze on surfaces it encounters, and this may be a more valid cause than radiative cooling. Because this happened with ships' anchors, this ice is called anchor ice. Spray from turbulent streams and waterfalls can also freeze as rime ice on objects near the water.

Hail is a polycrystalline mass of snow crystals that have clumped together, partially melted, and then have been refrozen in updrafts, so that there may be an onion-like layered structure. It comes in a great range of sizes, but large hail is fortunately rare, because it is very destructive. Most hail is marble-sized or smaller. If the clumps have not been refrozen, the result is the soft masses called graupel. The white color is again due to scattering by the minute surface irregularities. Snow that falls goes through a regular series of changes depending on time and temperature that turn it into grainy névé or firn, and finally into solid ice, unless it melts first. Fresh snow has a density of about 0.1 g/cc (that is, 10" of snow make 1" of water), old snow about 0.4 or 0.5 g/cc.

At -15 °C, ice has a coeffient of linear expansion along the c-axis of 46 x 10-6 per K, and perpendicular to the c-axis 63 x 10-6 per K, for a coefficient of volume expansion of ß = 156 x 10-6 per K. At 0 °C, ß is about 200 x 10-6 per K. The latent heat of fusion is 79.72 cal/g, and the latent heat of sublimation is 678 cal/g, at 0 °C. The specific heat at constant pressure is 0.505 cal/g/K at 0 °C. The Debye temperature is 315K, from which the specific heat at low temperatures can be estimated. The heat conductivity of ice is 0.0057 cal/s/cm/K, about the same as many rocks, and 1/100 of that of aluminium. The thermal conductivity of water at 12 °C is 0.00136 for comparison, about a quarter that of ice. New snow with a density of 0.11 g/cc has a conductivity of 0.00256, but old snow with d = 0.45 has 0.000115, a counter-intuitive figure, but that is what the reference (Lange's Handbook of Chemistry) says. Perhaps old snow has voids filled with air that reduce the conductivity. In any case, snow or ice acts as an insulating blanket. This is no secret to the people who live in igloos.

The adiabatic bulk modulus of ice at -13 °C is 7.81 x 1010 dyne/cm^2. If the Poisson's ratio is assumed to be 1/3, then the shear modulus is 2.93 x 1010 dyne/cm^2, and Young's modulus is 7.81 x 1010 dyne/cm^2 or 1133 ksi. This means ice is much more springy than steel or aluminium. The speed of longitudinal sound waves is 2919 m/s, and shear waves will travel at 1788 m/s. I have not been able to find information on the compressional or tensile strength of ice on the Internet, or anywhere else for that matter, but these things are not difficult to measure, and must certainly be known. In fact, ice information in general is not as easy to find as one would expect for such an important and familiar substance. Ice has indeed been used as a material of construction, as in the Ice Palace of Leadville, and roads and railways have been built across it, as across the frozen Susquehanna before there was a bridge. Ice sculpture is a winter entertainment.

Structure of Ice

Ice has the chemical composition H_2O, molecular weight 18.016 11.2% hydrogen and 88.2% oxygen, by weight. It is a lattice of oxygen atoms, a macromolecule, held together by curious bonds consisting of a proton and two electrons joining O^{+}+ ions, arranged tetrahedrally. The bond length is 0.276 nm, with the proton closer to one oxygen than to the other, at distances 0.100 nm and 0.176 nm. This is a hydrogen bond, an interesting feature of water substance in all its forms.

It is fortunate for us that the earth is so massive, since the water molecule is light, and can easily escape the gravitational attraction of a planet. This has happened on Mars to such an extent that water no longer occurs in its atmosphere or surface. Buried ice holds what remains. Although signs of buried ice have been reported, no ice has yet been discovered. The surface of Mars seems to display evidence of earlier water on the planet, however. Without water, weathering is very slow on Mars. Life on Mars probably disappeared with the water. The earth is still covered with a thin sheet of water, water-ice weathering is active, and life continues.

The crystal structure of ice is well-known, and its properties can be calculated from the known structure, in contrast to water, for which the structure is still imperfectly known. (The normal modes of vibration, however, have not been determined.) Bragg inferred the positions of the oxygens by X-ray diffraction in 1922, and neutron scattering later located the protons.

If two electrons are taken away from an oxygen atom, the resulting O^{++} is isoelectronic with C, and its four valence electrons can form four tetrahedral bonds at angles of 109.5°. Of course, this ion does not actually exist and its charges are compensated by other electrons, but it is a good starting point for understanding the structure of ice. From the example of diamond, one might expect the oxygens to form a diamond lattice whose free energy would be less than that of the alternatives. In fact, ice Ic has just this structure, and is still lighter than water. Another possibility is the formation of six-membered rings. With carbon, the great stability of the benzene ring makes graphite the stable form under normal conditions. This is impossible for oxygens and hydrogen bonds, however, so there can be no graphitic ice. However, carbon does form stable, unstrained six-membered rings in cyclohexane, and this oxygens and hydrogen bonds can do.

The view at the left may help. It shows the hexagonal passages through the crystal parallel to the c-axis, the axis of symmetry. The crystal consists of puckered sheets of oxygens that stack so that the passages are preserved. The model has three such sheets. Alternate sheets are rotated by 60° about the c-axis. In each sheet, every oxygen has its fourth bond, the one that bonds the sheets to each other, either upward or downward, alternately. See if you can recognize this "bed of nails" in the photos. It is easier to do this in the top photo. One bond is alternately up and down in neighboring oxygens. Now note how the vertical bonds align in successive sheets, so that the distances between unbonded oxygens are alternately long and short. The oxygens are arranged like the carbons in the "chair" form of cyclohexane, but the seat of the chair is not horizontal. It would be interesting to discover a carbon allotrope with this structure—it would be a clear, softer form of diamond. Apparently, the urge to collapse into benzene rings is too strong to overcome.

Now we can put in the hydrogen bonds. Between each oxygen ion go a proton and two electrons, which makes the lattice electrically neutral. The electron on each side of the proton teams up with a valence electron on the oxygen ion to pair up in a bonding orbital. Instead of a symmetrical bond with two rather weak single bonds between the proton and each oxygen (hydrogen does not really feel comfortable when divalent), the lowest free energy results when one bond is a strong single bond of length 0.100 nm, while the other is a weaker bond of length 0.176 nm. The proton can pop from one location to the other if it can surmount the low potential barrier. However, for stability every oxygen is surrounded by two short bonds and two long ones. This means that at every oxygen, a water molecule can be identified. However, these water molecules are not permanent, but in a state of constant change as the protons pop back and forth in twos. If there are N oxygens, the number of ways the protons can be arranged is (3/2)N, which makes an observable contribution to the entropy of Nk ln(3/2) = 0.81 cal/mol/K.

The angle between the hydrogens is 105.5° in the water molecule, and the bond length is 0.0965 nm. In ice, the tetrahedral angle of 109.5° and the bond length of 0.100 nm are not much different. Therefore, there can be assumed to be an undistorted water molecule at each oxygen.

Like water, ice has a large polarizability because of the mobile protons. In a single crystal, the dielectric constant parallel to the c-axis is about 105 at 0 °C, and perpendicular it is about 92. The dielectric relaxation time at 0 °C is about 20 μs, corresponding to a frequency of 7.96 kHz. For comparison, in water the relaxation time is about 1.78×10^{-12} s, and the corresponding frequency is 89 GHz. A microwave oven heats water readily by dipole moment relaxation, but ice remains cold. At higher frequencies, the dielectric constant is about 3.1, with contributions now from molecular vibration. At still higher frequencies, the dielectric constant becomes about 1.7, in line with the optical index of refraction. Ice is a positive uniaxial crystal, with n^o = 1.3090 and n^e = 1.3104. This is a very small birefringence, and in most cases the index can be taken as 1.310, and the crystal as isotropic.

Ice in the Sky

In the standard atmosphere, 0 °C is reached at an altitude of 2300 m or 7550 ft. At the tropopause, 11 km altitude, the temperature is -56 °C. Therefore, through much of the lower atmosphere, ice is the stable form of water. It has always been a hazard to aeronautics, from ice forming in the Venturi of a carburetor (now a past hazard in most cases) to ice coating lifting surfaces. Ice is rare at higher altitudes, so it is mostly a mid-altitude problem. Supersaturated air can quickly deposit a coating of ice when encouraged by the presence of the surface. It is difficult to get a water droplet or an ice crystal started unless the supersaturation is large or the temperature very low, so generally they form of condensation nuclei, which are small clusters of charged ions.

Middle-level clouds (3-7 km) may be partly or entirely ice clouds, while high-level clouds (7-11 km) are entirely ice clouds. Observing cloud forms, and the precipitating crystals that fall in streams from them, is a pleasant diversion. Condensation trails from high aircraft are also formed from ice crystals that have condensed from the moisture in the engine exhaust. Optical phenomena are seen mainly in light that has passed through thin, high clouds, usually classed as cirrostratus. Often the cloud itself cannot be seen except for the scattered and refracted light that it has modified.

The commonest phenomenon is the corona of scattered light that surrounds any bright celestial body, usually the moon. If the cloud particles are small, a micron in diameter or smaller, and well-sorted by size, colors due to interference may be seen. This is a result of only the size of the particles, and it does not matter whether they are ice, water or smoke. Usually just a fuzzy ring can be seen, only a degree or so in diameter.

More rarely the particles are hexagonal columns of random orientation, and refraction by these columns causes halo phenomena, which are always impressive. Halo phenomena might be considered common (in some places they occur more than 200 days of the year) if you watched the sky continuously, but random glances for a few minutes are very likely to miss them. However, a look at the moon near full and not too high in the sky will show you lunar halos at least a few times every year, especially when you look at times when high cirrus clouds have been noted during the day. Solar haloes are brighter, and may show rarer phenomena, but seem very much more difficult to see than lunar haloes. Haloes are more easily seen if the direct view of the sun is blocked by a building or similar screen.

The best time to see solar halos is in the late afternoon when cirrostratus is about, and the most frequent phenomenon (at least in Denver) are the sun dogs, mock suns or parhelia a little more than 22° to the right and left of the sun. They correspond to capped columns falling with vertical axes, which is the orientation assumed by such falling crystals because of the cap. The sun dogs are just bright spots to each side the halo. They are actually outside the 22° halo, further away as the sun is higher, sometimes joined to it by a tangential arc, the arc of Lowitz. There are rarer phenomena, such as the 46 & dg; halo, the 90° halo, the parhelic circle, the circumscribed halo, and others. Most of these can now be calculated by computer programs, but mysteries and controversies still exist, especially as to causes.

The path of a light ray through a principal plane of a hexagonal crystal is shown at the right. It is much more difficult to handle rays that do not lie in a plane normal to the axis, but it can be done if necessary. We are looking only for approximate results, so this is a reasonable simplification. Snell's Law is applied at the entry and exit points, so sin i = n sin r and n sin i′ = sin r. The angles r and i′ are connected by A = r + i′. Starting with a certain angle of incidence i, r is first calculated, then i′ is found, and finally the angle r. The deviation of the ray is D = i - r + r′ - i′, or D = i + r′ - A.

If you carry out the calculation for a few values of i, you will find that the deviation passes through a minimum Dm. This happens when the path of the ray is symmetrical, so that r = i′ = A/2. Then, i and r′ are equal as well, and i = r′ = $(D_m + A)/2$. By Snell's law, sin i = n sin r, or sin $[(D_m + A)/2]$ = n sin A/2, from which n = sin $[(D_m + A)/2]$ / sin A/2, so that the index of refraction can be found if the angle of minimum deviation has been measured.

In the present case, A = 60° and n = 1.310. If we solve for D_m, we find 21.84°, or about 22°. Now consider refraction from numerous crystals oriented at random. None of these will refract light with a deviation less than the minimum, so we will get no light from the crystals within a cone of 22° about the direction of, say, the moon. Outside of this cone, various crystals at all points will send some light to us. In most cases, the deviation will not be far from the minimum, so the light will concentrate around 22°, and become less at larger angles. This is, in fact, what is observed. The halo has a sharp inner edge and a diffuse outer edge. We will see part of the halo wherever there are crystals in that direction. Since the index of refraction varies with frequency, the angle will be slightly smaller for red light, so there may be a reddish inner border. Outside of this, the colours will fall on one another, and there will be no color. This, also agrees with observation. The rainbow also is a result of refraction, but at the angle of minimum deviation for a refracting sphere there is the interference of two waves that produces peaks in the intensity, and so we see bright colors. In this case, there are no peaks, so colors are absent.

6 Self-ionization of Water

The self-ionization of water (also autoionization of water, and autodissociation of water) is the chemical reaction in which two water molecules react to produce a hydronium ion (H_3O^+) and a hydroxide ion (OH^-):

$$2\ H_2O\ (l)\ \rightleftarrows\ DH_3O^+\ (aq) + OH^-\ (aq)$$

It is an example of autoprotolysis, and relies on the amphoteric nature of water.

Water, however pure, is not a simple collection of H_2O molecules. Even in "pure" water, sensitive equipment can detect a very slight electrical conductivity of 0.055 $\mu S{\cdot}cm^{-1}$. According to the theories of Svante Arrhenius, this must be due to the presence of ions.

Concentration and Frequency

The preceding reaction has a chemical equilibrium constant of $K_{eq} = ([H_3O^+]\ [OH^-])/[H_2O]^2 = 3.23 \times 10^{-18}$. So the acidity constant which is $K_a = K_{eq} \times [H_2O] = ([H_3O^+]\ [OH^-])/[H_2O] = 1.8 \times 10\text{-}16$. For reactions in water (or diluted aqueous solutions), the molarity (a unit of concentration) of water, $[H_2O]$, is practically constant and is omitted from the acidity constant expression by convention. The resulting equilibrium constant is called the ionization constant, dissociation constant, or self-ionization constant, or ion product of water and is symbolized by K_w.

$$K_w = K_a\,[H_2O] = K_{eq}\,[H_2O]^2 = [H_3O^+]\,[OH^-]$$

where

$[H_3O^+]$ = molarity of hydrogen or hydronium ion, and

$[OH^-]$ = molarity of hydroxide ion.

At Standard Ambient Temperature and Pressure (SATP), about 25 °C (298 K), $K_w = [H_3O^+][OH^-] = 1.0 \times 10^{-14}$. Pure water ionizes or dissociates into equal amounts of H_3O^+ and OH^-, so their molarities are equal:

$[H_3O^+] = [OH^-]$.

At SATP, the concentrations of hydroxide and hydronium are both very low at 1.0×10^{-7} mol/L and the ions are rarely produced: a randomly selected water molecule will dissociate within approximately 10 hours Since the concentration of water molecules in water is largely unaffected by dissociation and $[H_2O]$ equals approximately 56 mol/l, it follows that for every 5.6×108 water molecules, one pair will exist as ions. Any solution in which the H_3O^+ and OH^- concentrations equal each other is considered a neutral solution. Absolutely pure water is neutral, although even trace amounts of impurities could affect these ion concentrations and the water may no longer be neutral. K_w is sensitive to both pressure and temperature; it increases when either increases.

It should be noted that deionized water (also called DI water) is water that has had most *impurity* ions common in tap water or natural water sources (such as Na^+ and Cl^-) removed by means of distillation or some other water purification method. Removal of *all* ions from water is next to impossible, since water self-ionizes quickly to reach equilibrium.

Dependence on Temperature and Pressure

By definition, $pK_w = -\log_{10} K_w$. At SATP, $pK_w = -\log_{10} (1.0\times10^{-14}) = 14.0$. The value of pK_w varies with temperature. As temperature increases, pK_w decreases; and as temperature decreases, pK_w increases (for temperatures up to about 250 °C). This means that ionization of water typically increases with temperature.

There is also a (usually small) dependence on pressure (ionization increases with increasing pressure). The dependence of the water ionization on temperature and pressure has been well investigated and a standard formulation exists.

Acidity

pH is a logarithmic measure of the acidity (or alkalinity) of an aqueous solution. By definition, $pH = -\log_{10} [H_3O^+]$. Since $[H_3O^+] = [OH^-]$ in a neutral solution, by mathematics, for a neutral aqueous solution pH = 7 at SATP.

Self-ionization is the process that determines the pH of water. Since the concentration of hydronium at SATP (approximately 25 °C) is 1.0×10^{-7}mol/l, the pH of pure liquid water at this temperature is 7. Since K_w increases as temperature increases, hot water has a higher concentration of hydronium than cold water, but this does not mean it is more acidic, as the hydroxide concentration is also higher by the same amount.

Mechanism

The electric field fluctuations in liquid water cause molecular dissociation. They propose the following sequence of events that takes place in about 150 fs (A festo second (fs) is the SI unit of time equal to 10^{-15} of a sec) the system begins in a neutral state; random fluctuations in molecular motions occasionally (about once every 10 hours per water molecule) produce an electric field strong enough to break an oxygen-hydrogen bond, resulting in a hydroxide (OH^-) and hydronium ion (H_3O^+); the proton of the hydronium ion travels along water molecules by the Grotthuss mechanism; and a change in the hydrogen bond network in the solvent isolates the two ions, which are stabilized by solvation.

Within 1 picosecond, however, a second reorganization of the hydrogen bond network allows rapid proton transfer down the electric potential difference and subsequent recombination of the ions. This time scale is consistent with the time it takes for hydrogen bonds to reorient themselves in water.

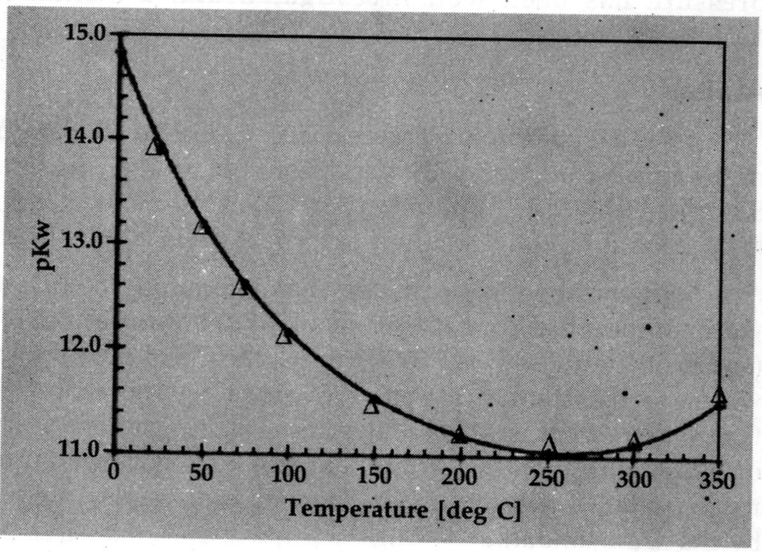

Fig. 6.1

Pressure dependence of the water ionization constant at 25 °C

Isotope Effects

Heavy water, D_2O, self-ionizes less than normal water, H_2O; oxygen forms a slightly stronger bond to deuterium because the larger mass of deuterium difference results in a lower zero-point energy, a quantum mechanical effect. The following table compares the values of pK_w for H_2O and D_2O.

Ions in Water Solution

Before we can get into the thermodynamics of electrochemistry we have to take a look at how we deal with the chemical potentials of ions in water solution. For example, we know that soluble ionic compounds are completely ionized in water,

$$NaCl(aq) \rightarrow Na^+(aq) + Cl^-(aq). \quad (6.1)$$

(A better way to say this is that when ionic compounds dissolve they are completely dissociated into ions. This way of stating it includes compounds like AgCl, which are not regarded as soluble ionic compounds, but do give very small concentrations of ions in water solution.)

The chemical potentials must be consistent with the formation of ions,

$$\mu_{NaCl(aq)} = \mu_{Na+(aq)} + \mu_{cl-(aq)} \quad (6.2)$$

which also implies that

$$\mu^o{}_{NaCl(aq)} = \mu^o{}_{Na+(aq)} + \mu^o{}_{Cl-(aq)} \quad (6.3)$$

We also know that we can (must?) write

$$\mu_{NaCl(aq)} = \mu^o{}_{NaCl(aq)} + RT\ 1n\ a_{NaCl(aq)} \quad (6.4)$$

When working with ionic solutions we would like to be a little more specific about the activities of the species in solution. It is customary to use units of molality, *m*, for ions and compounds in water solution. If the solutions were ideal we could write

$$a_i = m_i, \quad (6.5)$$

and the chemical potential would be written

$$\mu_i = \mu^o_i + RT\ln m_i \tag{6.6}$$

Two things must be said about this equation. First, it must be understood that there is an implied m^o_i dividing the m_i inside the logarithm, and second, the standard state is the solution at concentration $m_i = m^o_i$. Usually we set $m^o_i = 1$ molal.

However, ionic solutions are far from ideal so we must correct this expression for chemical potential for the nonidealities. As usual, we will use an activity coefficient , and write the activity as

$$m_i\, \gamma_i / m^o_i,$$

and consistent with what we have been doing, we will set m^o_i to 1 molal and not write it in the equation. Thus the chemical potential will be written

$$\mu i = \mu^o i + RT\ln m_i\gamma_i \tag{6.7}$$

The standard state for this equation is a hypothetical standard state. The standard state is not actually realizable. We are using the so-called Henry's law standard state in which the solution obey's Henry's law in the limit of infinite dilution. That is,

$$\text{"}\gamma i\text{"} \rightarrow 1 \text{ in the limit when } m_i \rightarrow 0. \tag{6.8}$$

(There most likely is a concentration where $m_i\, \gamma_i = 1$, but, interestingly enough that would not be the standard state. The fact that at that concentration the chemical potential would equal the chemical potential of the standard state is a coincidence.)

In what follows we will rarely, if ever, deal with more than one positive and one negative ionic species in the solution. In this case we will simplify matters by writing

$$m_+ \,,\ \gamma_+ \text{ and } m_- \,,\ \gamma_-$$

for the molalities and activity coefficients of the positive and negative ionic species, respectively.

We will also refer to the ionic compound simply as the "salt." With this notation we can rewrite Eq. (6.2) as,

$$\mu_{salt} = \mu_+ + \mu_- \tag{6.9}$$

or

$$\begin{aligned}
&\mu^o_{\text{salt}} + RT1\text{n } a_{\text{salt}} \\
&= \mu^o_+ RT1\text{n } m_+ \gamma_+ + \mu^o_- + RT1\text{n } m_- \gamma_- \\
&= \mu^o_+ + \mu^o_{..} + RT1\text{n } m_+ g + m_- \gamma_- \\
&= \mu^o_+ + \mu^o_- + RT1\text{n } m_+ m_- \gamma_+ \gamma_-
\end{aligned} \tag{6.10}$$

Eq. (6.9) is also true when all the components are in their standard states, so we can write,

$$\mu^o_{\text{salt}} = \mu^o_+ + \mu^o_- \tag{6.11}$$

Combining eq. (6.10) and (6.11) we see that

$$\begin{aligned}
RT1\text{n } a_{salt} &= RT1\text{n} m_+ \gamma_+ + RT1\text{n } m_- \gamma_- \\
&= RT1\text{n } m_+ \gamma_+ m_- \gamma_- \\
&= RT1\text{n } m_+ m_- \gamma_+ \gamma_-
\end{aligned} \tag{6.12}$$

from which we conclude that

$$a_{salt} = m_+ m_- \gamma_+ \gamma_- \tag{6.13}$$

The activity coefficients, γ_+ and γ_- can't be measured independently because solutions must be electrically neutral. In other words, you can't make a solution which has just positive or just negative ions. You can't calculate the individual activity coefficients from theory, either. However, you can measure a "geometric mean" activity coefficient and, within limits, you can calculate it from theory. (We will show how to do both of these things later.) The actual form of the geometric mean depends on the number of ions produced by the salt. Right now we will define it for NaCl and then give more examples later. For NaCl we define,

$$\gamma_+\gamma_- = \gamma^2_\pm \quad (6.14)$$

But for a NaCl solution of molality, *m*, we have $m_+ = m$ and $m_- = m$ so that

$$a_{salt} = m^2\gamma^2_\pm \quad (6.15)$$

Keep in mind that this for is for NaCl, but it is correct for any one-to-one ionic compound.

Try $MgCl_2$,

$$MgCl_2 \; ? \; Mg^{2+} + 2\,Cl^- \quad (6.16)$$

$$\mu^o_{salt} + RT1n\; a_{salt}$$

$$= \mu^o_{Mg2+} + RT1n\; m_{Mg2+}\,\gamma_+ + 2\mu^o_- + 2\,RT1n\; m_{cl}-\gamma-$$

$$= \mu^o_+ + 2\mu^o_- + RT1n\; m_+\gamma_+m^2-\gamma^2-$$

$$= \mu^o_{salt} + RT1n\; m_+m^2_-\gamma_+\gamma^2_- \quad (6.17)$$

so

$$a_{salt} = m_+m^2_-\gamma+\gamma^2_- \quad (6.18)$$

But for $MgCl_2$ at molality, *m*, we know that $m_+ = m$ and $m_- = 2m$. Further, we define the geometric mean activity coefficient by,

$$\gamma_\pm = (\gamma+\gamma^2_-)^{1/3} \quad (6.19)$$

Then

$$a_{salt} = m(2m)^2\,\gamma^3_\pm = 4m^3\gamma^3_\pm \quad (6.20)$$

Let's do one more, LaCl3.

$$LaCl_3 \rightarrow La^{3+} + 3\,Cl^- \quad (6.21)$$

$$\mu^o_{salt} + RT1na_{salt} = \mu^o_{La3+}\gamma_+ + 3\mu^o_- + 3RT1n\; m_{cl-}\gamma_-$$

$$= \mu^o_+ + 3\mu^o_- + RT\;1nm_+\,\gamma_+m^3-\gamma^3_-$$

$$= \mu^o_{salt} + RT\;1n\; m_+m^3_-\gamma_+\gamma^3_- \quad (6.22)$$

so

$$a_{salt} = m_+m^3_-\gamma_+\gamma^3_- \quad (6.23)$$

But for $LaCl_3$ at molality, m, we know that $m_+ = m$ and $m_- = 3m$. Further, we define the geometric mean activity coefficient by,

$$\gamma_\pm = (\gamma_+\gamma_-^3)^{1/4} \tag{6.24}$$

Then

$$a_{salt} = m(3m)^3\gamma_\pm^4 = 27m^4\gamma_\pm^4 \tag{6.25}$$

Other ionic compounds are done in a similar manner. After some practice you can probably figure out the expression for assault just by looking at the compound. Until then, or when in doubt, go back to the expressions for chemical potentials as we have done here. [For practice you might want to try $Al_2(SO_4)_3$.] We will apply all of this by looking at the:

Relationship between $K_{thermodynamic}$ and $K_{molality}$

Use an example to show this relationship;

$$AgCl(s) \rightarrow Ag^+(aq) + Cl^-(aq). \tag{6.26}$$

$$K_{them\,o} = \frac{a_+a_-}{1} = m_+\gamma_+m_-\gamma_-^{\bullet}$$
$$= m_+m_-\gamma_\pm^2 \tag{6.27}$$

Then,

$$m_+m_- = \frac{K_{them\,o}}{\gamma_\pm^2} = K_{sp} \tag{6.28}$$

If we are just dealing with AgCl in water the concentrations of the ions are pretty small so $\gamma_\pm$ is approximately unity. If, however, we are dealing with the common ion effect, for example, the solubility of AgCl in 0.10 m HCl, then the $\gamma_\pm$ for the ions in this stronger solution is not equal to one, not even approximately so.

Which takes us to the:

Debye-Hückel Limiting Law (DHLL)

Theoretical calculation of $\gamma_{\pm}$.

The Debye Hückel limiting law gives the g± in terms of the *ionic strength, I,* defined as,

$$I = \frac{1}{2}\sum_i m_i z_i^2 \tag{6.29}$$

where z_i is the charge on ion i, and m_i is the molality of ion i.

Examples,

0.010 m HCL

$$I = \frac{1}{2}\left(0.01(+1)^2 + 0.01(-1)^2\right) = 0.10 \tag{6.30}$$

$$I = \frac{1}{2}\left(0.20(+1)^2 + 0.10(-2)^2\right)$$

$$= \frac{1}{2}(0.20 + 0.40) \tag{6.31}$$

$$= 0.30 \text{ molal}$$

We must include all ions in the solution. The ionic strength is a measure of the total concentration of charge in the solution. Notice that it includes contributions from both the number of ions in the solution and the charges on the individual ions. Look at Eq. 31 to see how the -2 charge on the SO_4^{2-} ion contributes to the ionic strength.

Test yourself on $LaCl_3$.

We won't derive the Debye-Hückel Limiting Law. We will just give the result without proof. DHLL says,

$$1n\gamma_{\pm} = -1.177\,|\,z_+z_-\,|\sqrt{1} \tag{6.32}$$

A more accurate version is,

$$\ln \gamma_{\pm} = \frac{-1.177\,|\,z_{+}z_{-}\,|\sqrt{I}}{1+Ba_{0}\sqrt{I}} \approx \frac{-1.177\,|\,z_{+}z_{-}\,|\sqrt{I}}{1+\sqrt{I}} \tag{6.33}$$

The *B* and *a*o are parameters from the details of the theoretical model, such as the dielectric constant of water, sizes of ions, and so on.

It is not unusual to see common logarithms used instead of natural logarithms, as in,

$$\log \gamma_{\pm} = -0.509\,|\,Z_{+}Z_{-}\,|\sqrt{I} \tag{6.34}$$

and its other variations given above. I suspect that this is because, before the advent of electronic calculators, people used tables of common logarithms to carry out calculations involving many multiplications and divisions.

7 Hard Water

Hard water is the type of water that has high mineral content (in contrast with *soft water*). Hard water minerals primarily consist of calcium (Ca^{2+}), and magnesium (Mg^{2+}) metal cations, and sometimes other dissolved compounds such as bicarbonates and sulfates. Calcium usually enters the water as either calcium carbonate ($CaCO_3$), in the form of limestone and chalk, or calcium sulfate ($CaSO_4$), in the form of other mineral deposits. The predominant source of magnesium is dolomite ($CaMg(CO_3)_2$). Hard water is generally not harmful.

The simplest way to determine the hardness of water is the lather/froth test: soap or toothpaste, when agitated, lathers easily in soft water but not in hard water. More exact measurements of hardness can be obtained through a wet titration. The total water 'hardness' (including both Ca^{2+} and Mg^{2+} ions) is read as parts per million (ppm) or weight/volume (mg/L) of calcium carbonate ($CaCO_3$) in the water. Although water hardness usually only measures the total concentrations of calcium and magnesium (the two most prevalent, divalent metal ions), iron, aluminium, and manganese may also be present at elevated levels in some geographical locations.

Hardness

Hardness in water is defined as the presence of multivalent cations. Hardness in water can cause water to form scales and a resistance to soap. It can also be defined as water that doesn't produce lather with soap solutions, but produces white precipitate (scum). Example :

$$2C_{17}H_{35}COONa + Ca^{2+} \rightarrow (C_{17}H_{35}COO)_2Ca + 2Na^+$$

Types of Hard Water

In the 1960s, scientist Chris Gilby discovered that hard water can be categorized by the ions found in the water. A distinction is also made between 'temporary' and 'permanent' hard water.

Temporary Hardness

Temporary hardness is caused by a combination of calcium ions and bicarbonate ions in the water. It can be removed by boiling the water or by the addition of lime (calcium hydroxide). Boiling promotes the formation of carbonate from the bicarbonate and precipitates calcium carbonate out of solution, leaving water that is softer upon cooling.

The following is the equilibrium reaction when calcium carbonate ($CaCO_3$) is dissolved in water:

$$CaCO_3(s) + H_2CO_3(aq) \rightleftharpoons Ca^{2+}(aq) + 2HCO_3^-(aq)$$

Upon heating, less CO_2 is able to dissolve into the water (see Solubility). Since there is not enough CO_2 around, the reaction cannot proceed from left to right, and therefore the $CaCO_3$ will not dissolve as rapidly. Instead, the reaction is forced to the left (i.e. products to reactants) to re-establish equilibrium, and solid $CaCO_3$ is formed. Boiling the water will remove hardness as long as the solid $CaCO_3$ that precipitates out is removed. After cooling, if enough time passes the water will pick up CO_2 from the air and the reaction will again proceed from left to right, allowing the $CaCO_3$ to "re-dissolve" into the water.

The solubility of calcium carbonate in water and how it is affected by atmospheric carbon dioxide, see calcium carbonate.

Permanent Hardness

Permanent hardness is hardness (mineral content) that cannot be removed by boiling. It is usually caused by the presence of calcium and magnesium sulfates and/or chlorides in the water, which become more soluble as the temperature rises. Despite the name, permanent hardness can be removed using a water softener or ion exchange column, where the calcium and magnesium ions are exchanged with the sodium ions in the column. Hard water causes scaling, which is the left over mineral deposits that are formed after the hard water had evaporated. This is also known as limescale.

The scale can clog pipes, ruin water heaters, coat the insides of tea and coffee pots, and decrease the life of toilet flushing units. Similarly, insoluble salt residues that remain in hair after shampooing with hard water tend to leave hair rougher and harder to untangle. In industrial settings, water hardness must be constantly monitored to avoid costly breakdowns in boilers, cooling towers, and other equipment that comes in contact with water. Hardness is controlled by the addition of chemicals and by large-scale softening with zeolite and ion exchange resins.

Measurement

It is possible to measure the level of hard water by obtaining a free water testing kit. These are supplied by most water softening companies. There are several different scales used to describe the hardness of water in different contexts.

- Parts per million (ppm)

  Usually defined as one milligram of calcium carbonate ($CaCO_3$) per litre of water.

- grains/gallon (gpg)

  Defined as 1 grain (64.8 mg) of calcium carbonate per U.S. gallon (3.79 litres), or 17.118 ppm

- mmol/L (millimoles per litre)

  One millimole of calcium (either Ca^{2+} or $CaCO_3$) per litre of water corresponds to a hardness of 100.09 ppm or 5.608 dGH, since the molar mass of calcium carbonate is 100.09 g/mol.

- Degrees of General Hardness (dGH)

  One degree of General Hardness is defined as 10 milligrams of calcium oxide per litre of water, which is the same as one German degree (17.848 ppm).

- Various obsolete "degrees"
- Clark degrees (°Clark)/English degrees (°E)

  One degree Clark is defined as one grain (64.8 mg) of calcium carbonate per Imperial gallon (4.55 litres) of water, equivalent to 14.254 ppm.

- German degrees (*Deutsche Härte,* °dH)

  One degree German is defined as 10 milligrams of calcium oxide per litre of water. This is equivalent to 17.848 milligrams of calcium carbonate per litre of water, or 17.848 ppm.

- French degrees (°f) (letter to be written in lowercase to avoid confusion with degree Fahrenheit — not always adhered to) one degree French is defined as 10 milligrams of calcium carbonate per litre of water, equivalent to 10 ppm.

- American degrees

  One degree American is defined as one milligram of calcium carbonate per litre of water, equivalent to 1 ppm.

Although most of the above measures define hardness in terms of concentrations of calcium in water, any combination of calcium and magnesium cations having the same total molarity as a pure calcium solution will yield the same degree of hardness. Consequently, hardness concentrations for naturally occurring waters (which will contain both Ca^{2+} and Mg^{2+} ions), are usually expressed as an equivalent concentration of pure calcium in solution. For example, water that contains 1.5 mmol/L of elemental calcium (Ca^{2+}) and 1.0 mmol/L of magnesium (Mg^{2+}) is equivalent in hardness to a 2.5 mmol/L solution of calcium alone (250.2 ppm).

Because it is the precise mixture of minerals dissolved in the water, together with the water's pH and temperature, that determines the behaviour of the hardness, a single-number scale does not adequately describe hardness. Descriptions of hardness correspond roughly with ranges of mineral concentrations:

- Very soft: 0-70 ppm, 0-4 dGH
- Soft: 70-140 ppm, 4-8 dGH
- Slightly hard: 140-210 ppm, 8-12 dGH
- Moderately hard: 210-320 ppm, 12-18 dGH
- Hard: 320-530 ppm, 18-30 dGH
- Very hard >530 ppm, >30 dGH

Indices

Several indices are used to describe the behaviour of calcium carbonate in water, oil, or gas mixtures.

Langelier Saturation Index (LSI)

The Langelier Saturation Index (sometimes Langelier Stability Index) is a calculated number used to predict the calcium carbonate stability of water. It indicates whether the water will precipitate, dissolve, or be in equilibrium with calcium carbonate. Langelier developed a method for predicting the pH at which water is saturated in calcium carbonate (called pHs). The LSI is expressed as the difference between the actual system pH and the saturation pH.

LSI = pH (measured) - pHs

- For LSI > 0, water is super saturated and tends to precipitate a scale layer of $CaCO_3$
- For LSI = 0, water is saturated (in equilibrium) with $CaCO_3$. A scale layer of $CaCO_3$ is neither precipitated nor dissolved.
- For LSI < 0, water is under saturated and tends to dissolve solid $CaCO_3$

If the actual pH of the water is below the calculated saturation pH, the LSI is negative and the water has a very limited scaling potential. If the actual pH exceeds pHs, the LSI is positive, and being supersaturated with $CaCO_3$, the water has a tendency to form scale. At increasing positive index values, the scaling potential increases.

In practice, water with an LSI between -0.5 and +0.5 will not display enhanced mineral dissolving or scale forming properties. Water with an LSI below -0.5 tends to exhibit noticeably increased dissolving abilities while water with an LSI above +0.5 tends to exhibit noticeably increased scale forming properties.

It is also worth noting that the LSI is temperature sensitive. The LSI becomes more positive as the water temperature increases. This has particular implications in situations where well water is used. The temperature of the water when it first exits the well is often significantly lower than the temperature inside the building served by the well or at the laboratory where the LSI measurement is made.

Ryznar Stability Index (RSI)

The Ryznar stability index (RSI) uses a database of scale thickness measurements in municipal water systems to predict the effect of water chemistry.

Ryznar saturation index (RSI) was developed from empirical observations of corrosion rates and film formation in steel mains. Ryznar saturation index is defined as:

RSI = 2 pHs – pH (measured)

- For 6, 5 < RSI < 7 water is considered to be approximately at saturation equilibrium with calcium carbonate.
- For RSI > 8 water is under saturated and, therefore, would tend to dissolve any existing solid $CaCO_3$.
- For RSI < 6, 5 water tends to be scale forming.

Puckorius Scaling Index (PSI)

The Puckorius Scaling Index (PSI) uses slightly different parameters to quantify the relationship between the saturation state of the water and the amount of limescale deposited.

Other Indices

Other indices include the Larson-Skold Index the Stiff-Davis Index and the Oddo-Tomson Index.

Health Considerations

The World Health Organization (WHO) says that "there does not appear to be any convincing evidence that water hardness causes adverse health effects in humans."

Some studies have shown a weak inverse relationship between water hardness and cardiovascular disease in men, up to a level of 170 mg calcium carbonate per litre of water. The World Health Organization has reviewed the evidence and concluded the data were inadequate to allow for a recommendation for a level of hardness.

In a review that there is a good overview of the topic, and unlike the WHO, sets some recommendations for the maximum and minimum levels of calcium (40-80 ppm) and magnesium (20-30 ppm) in drinking water, and a total hardness expressed as the sum of the calcium and magnesium concentrations of 2-4 mmol/L.

Other studies have shown weak correlations between cardiovascular health and water hardness.

A UK nationwide study, funded by the Department of Health, is investigating anecdotal evidence that childhood eczema may by correlated with hard water.

Very soft water can corrode the metal pipes in which it is carried and as a result the water may contain elevated levels of cadmium, copper, lead and zinc.

SOFTENING

Process

A water softener, like a fabric softener, works on the principle of cation or ion exchange in which ions of the hardness minerals are exchanged for sodium or potassium ions, effectively reducing the concentration of hardness minerals to tolerable levels and thus making the water softer and giving it a smoother feeling omical way to soften household water is with an ion exchange water softener. This unit uses sodium chloride (table salt) to recharge beads made of the ion exchange resins that exchange hardness mineral ions for sodium ions. Artificial or natural zeolites can also be used. As the hard water passes through and around the beads, the hardness mineral ions are preferentially absorbed, displacing the sodium ions. This process is called ion exchange. When the bead or sodium zeolite has a low concentration of sodium ions left, it is exhausted, and can no longer soften water. The resin is recharged by flushing (often *back*-flushing) with saltwater. The high excess concentration of sodium ions alter the equilibrium between the ions in solution and the ions held on the surface of the resin, resulting in replacement of the hardness mineral ions on the resin or zeolite with sodium ions. The resulting saltwater and mineral ion solution is then rinsed away, and the resin is ready to start the process all over again. This cycle can be repeated many times.

The discharge of brine water during this regeneration process has been banned in some jurisdictions (notably California, USA) due to concerns about the environmental impact of the discharged sodium.

Potassium chloride (softener salt substitute) may also be used to regenerate the resin beads. It exchanges the hardness ions for potassium. It also will exchange naturally occurring sodium for potassium resulting in sodium-free soft water.

Some softening processes in industry use the same method, but on a much larger scale. These methods create an enormous amount of salty water that is costly to treat and dispose of.

Temporary hardness, caused by hydrogen carbonate (or bicarbonate) ions, can be removed by boiling. For example, calcium bicarbonate, often present in temporary hard water, may be boiled in a kettle to remove the hardness. In the process, a scale forms on the inside of the kettle in a process known as "furring". This scale is composed of calcium carbonate.

$$Ca(HCO_3)_2 \rightarrow CaCO_3 + CO_2 + H_2O$$

Hardness can also be reduced with a lime-soda ash treatment. This process, developed by Thomas Clark in 1841, involves the addition of slaked lime (calcium hydroxide — $Ca(OH)_2$) to a hard water supply to convert the hydrogen carbonate hardness to carbonate, which precipitates and can be removed by filtration:

$$Ca(HCO_3)_2 + Ca(OH)_2 \rightarrow 2CaCO_3 + 2H_2O$$

The addition of sodium carbonate also permanently softens hard water containing calcium sulfate, as the calcium ions form calcium carbonate which precipitates out and sodium sulfate is formed which is soluble. The calcium carbonate that is formed sinks to the bottom. Sodium sulfate has no effect on the hardness of water.

$$Na_2CO_3 + CaSO_4 \rightarrow Na_2SO_4 + CaCO_3$$

Effects on Skin

Some confusion may arise after a first experience with soft water. Hard water does not lather well with soap and leaves a "less than clean" feeling. Soft water lathers better than hard water but leaves a "slippery feeling" on the skin after use with soap. A certain water softener manufacturer contends that the "slippery feeling" after showering in soft water is due to "cleaner skin" and the absence of "friction-causing" soap scum.

However, the chemical explanation is that softened water, due to its sodium content, has a much reduced ability to combine with the soap film on your body and therefore, it is much more difficult to rinse off. Solutions are to use less soap or a synthetic liquid body wash.

Regional Information

Hard Water in Australia

Analysis of water hardness in major Australian cities by the Australian Water Association shows a range from very soft (Melbourne) to very hard (Adelaide). Total Hardness levels of Calcium Carbonate in ppm are: Canberra: 40 Melbourne: 10-26 Sydney: 39.4-60.1 Perth: 29-226 Brisbane: 100 Adelaide: 134-148 ; Hobart: 5.8-34.4 Darwin: 31.

Hard Water in Canada

Prairie provinces (mainly Saskatchewan and Manitoba) contain high quantities of calcium and magnesium, often as dolomite, which are readily soluble in the groundwater that contains high concentrations of trapped carbon dioxide from the last glaciation. In these parts of Canada, the total hardness in ppm of calcium carbonate equivalent frequently exceed 200 ppm, if groundwater is the only source of potable water. The west coast, by contrast, has unusually soft water, derived mainly from mountain lakes fed by glaciers and snowmelt.

Some typical values are: Calgary 165 ppm, Regina 202 ppm, Saskatoon < 140 ppm, Winnipeg 77 ppm, Toronto 121 ppm, Vancouver < 3 ppm, Charlottetown PEI 140-150 ppm.

Hard Water in England and Wales

Information from the British Drinking Water Inspectorate shows that drinking water in England is generally considered to be 'very hard', with most areas of England, particularly the East, exhibiting above 200 ppm for the calcium carbonate equivalent. Wales, Devon, Cornwall and parts of North-West England are softer water areas, and range from 0 to 200 ppm . In the brewing industry in England and Wales, water is often deliberately hardened with gypsum in the process of Burtonisation.

Hard Water in the United States

According to the United States Geological Survey, 89.3% of US hoes have hard water. The softest waters occur in parts of the Nw England, South Atlantic-Gulf, Pacific Northwest, and Hawaii regions. Moderately hard waters are common in many of the rivers of the Tennessee, Great Lakes, Pacific Northwest, and Alasa regions. Hard and very hard waters are found in some of the streams in most of the regions throughout the country. Hardest waters (greater than 1,000 ppm) are in streams in Texas, New Mexico, Kansas, Arizona, and southern California.

WATER QUALITY

Water quality is the physical, chemical and biological characteristics of water. It is most frequently used by reference to a set of standards against which compliance can be assessed. The most common standards used to assess water quality relate to drinking water, safety of human contact, and for health of ecosystems.

Standards

In the setting of standards, agencies make political and technical/scientific decisions about how the water will be used. In the case f natural water bodies, they also make some reasonable estimate of pristine conditions. Different uses raise different concerns and therefore different standards are considered. Natural water bodies will vary in response to environmental conditions. Environmental scientists work to understand how these systems function which in turn helps to identify the sources and fates of contaminants. Environmental lawyers and policy makers work to define legislation that ensure that water is maintained at an appropriate quality for its identified use.

The vast majority of surface water on the planet is neither potable nor toxic. This remains true even if sea water in the oceans (which is too salty to drink) isn't counted. Another general perception of water quality is that of a simple property that tells whether water is polluted or not. In fact, water quality is a very complex subject, in part because water is a complex medium intrinsically tied to the ecology of the Earth. Industrial pollution is a major cause of water pollution, as well as runoff from agricultural areas, urban stormwater runoff and discharge of treated and untreated sewage (especially in developing countries).

Categories

The parameters for water quality are determined by the intended use. Work in the area of water quality tends to be focused on water that is treated for human consumption or in the environment.

Human Consumption

Contaminants that may be in untreated water include microorganisms such as viruses and bacteria; inorganic contaminants such as salts and metals; pesticides and herbicides; organic chemical contaminants from industrial processes and petroleum use; and radioactive contaminants. Water quality depends on the local geology and ecosystem, as well as human uses such as sewage dispersion, industrial pollution, use of water bodies as a heat sink, and overuse (which may lower the level of the water).

In the United States, the U.S. Environmental Protection Agency (EPA) limits the amounts of certain contaminants in tap water provided by public water systems. The Safe Drinking Water Act authorizes EPA to issue two types of standards: primary standards regulate substances that potentially affect human health, and secondary standards prescribe aesthetic qualities, those that affect taste, odor, or appearance. The U.S. Food and Drug Administration (FDA) regulations establish limits for contaminants in bottled water that must provide the same protection for public health. Drinking water, including bottled water, may reasonably be expected to contain at least small amounts of some contaminants. The presence of these contaminants does not necessarily indicate that the water poses a health risk.

Some people use water purification technology to remove contamnants from the municipal water supply they get in their hoes, or from local pumps or bodies of water. For people who get water from a local stream, lake, or aquifer (well), their drinking water is not filtered by the local government.

Environmental Water Quality

Environmental water quality, also called *ambient water quality*, pertains to water bodies such as lakes, rivers, and oceans. Ambient water quality standards vary significantly due to different environmental conditions, ecosystems, and intended human uses. Toxic substances and high populations of certain microorganisms can present a health hazard for non-drinking purposes such as irrigation, swimming, fishing, rafting, boating, and industrial uses. These conditions may also affect wildlife which use the water for drinking or as a habitat. Modern water quality laws general specify protection of fishable/swimmable use and anti-degradation of current conditions.

There is some desire among the public to return water bodies to prisne, or pre-industrial conditions. Current environmental laws focus of the designation of uses and therefore allow for some water contamination as long as the particular type of contamination is not harmful to the designated uses. Given the landscape changes in the watersheds of many freshwater bodies, returning to pristine conditions would be a significant challenge. In these cases, environmental scientists focus on achieving goals for maintaining populations of endangered species and protecting human health.

Measurement

The complexity of water quality as a subject is reflected in the many types of measurements of water quality indicators. Some of the simple measurements listed below can be made on-site (temperature, pH, dissolved oxygen, conductivity), in direct contact with the water source in question. More complex measurements that must be made in a lab setting require a water sample to be collected, preserved, and analyzed at another location. Making these complex measurements can be expensive. Because direct measurements of water quality can be expensive, ongoing monitoring programs are typically conducted by government agencies. However, there are local volunteer programs and resources available for some general assessment. Tools available to the general public are on-site test kits commonly used for home fish tanks and biological assessments.

The following is a list of indicators often measured by situational category:

Drinking Water

- Alkalinity
- Colour of water
- pH
- Taste and odor (geosmin, 2-methylisoborneol (MIB), etc)
- Dissolved metals and salts (sodium, chloride, potassium, calcium, manganese, magnesium)
- Microorganisms such as fecal coliform bacteria (Escherichia coli), Cryptosporidium, and Giardia lamblia
- Dissolved metals and metalloids (lead, mercury, arsenic, etc.)
- Dissolved organics: colored dissolved organic matter (CDOM), dissolved organic carbon (DOC)
- Radon
- Heavy metals
- Pharmaceuticals
- Hormone analogs

Environmental

Chemical Assessment

- pH
- Conductivity
- Dissolved Oxygen (DO)
- nitrate-N
- Orthophosphates
- Chemical oxygen demand (COD)
- Biochemical oxygen demand (BOD)
- Pesticides

Physical Assessment

- Temperature
- Total suspended solids (TSS)
- Turbidity

Biological Assessment

Biological monitoring metrics have been developed in many places, and one widely used measure is the presence and abundance of members of the insect orders Ephemeroptera, Plecoptera and Trichoptera. (Common names are, respectively, Mayfly, Stonefly and Caddisfly.) EPT indexes will naturally vary from region to region, but generally, within a region, the greater the number of taxa from these orders, the better the water quality. EPA and other organizations in the United States offer guidance on developing a monitoring program and identifying members of these and other aquatic insect orders.

Individuals interested in monitoring water quality who cannot afford or manage lab scale analysis can also use biological indicators to get a general reading of water quality. One example is the IO water volunteer water monitoring program, which includes a benthic macro invertebrate indicator key.

8 Electrolysis of Water

Electrolysis of water is the decomposition of water (H_2O) into oxygen (O_2) and hydrogen gas (H_2) due to an electric current being passed through the water. This electrolytic process is used in some industrial applications when hydrogen is needed.

An electrical power source is connected to two electrodes, or two plates, (typically made from some inert metal such as platinum or stainless steel) which are placed in the water. Hydrogen will appear at the cathode (the negatively charged electrode, where electrons are pumped into the water), and oxygen will appear at the anode (the positively charged electrode). The generated amount of hydrogen is twice the amount of oxygen, and both are proportional to the total electrical charge that was sent through the water.

Electrolysis of pure water is very slow, and can only occur due to the self-ionization of water. Pure water has an electrical conductivity about one millionth that of seawater. It is sped up dramatically by adding an electrolyte (such as a salt, an acid or a base).

Historically, the first known electrolysis of water was done by William Nicholson and Anthony Carlisle in about 1800.

Equations

In the water at the negatively charged cathode, a reduction reaction takes place, with electrons (e-) from the cathode being given to hydrogen cations to form hydrogen gas (the half reaction balanced with acid):

Cathode (reduction): $2H^+(aq) + 2e^- \rightarrow H_2(g)$

At the positively charged anode, an oxidation reaction occurs, generating oxygen gas and giving electrons to the cathode to complete the circuit:

Anode (oxidation): $2H_2O(l) \rightarrow O_2(g) + 4H^+(aq) + 4e^-$

The same half reactions can also be balanced with base as listed below. Not all half reactions must be balanced with acid or base. Many do like the oxidation or reduction of water listed here. To add half reactions they must both be balanced with either acid or base.

Cathode (reduction): $2H_2O(l) + 2e^- \rightarrow H_2(g) + 2OH^-(aq)$

Anode (oxidation): $4OH^-(aq) \rightarrow O_2(g) + 2H_2O(l) + 4e^-$

Combining either half reaction pair yields the same overall decomposition of water into oxygen and hydrogen:

Overall reaction: $2H_2O(l) \rightarrow 2H_2(g) + O_2(g)$

The number of hydrogen molecules produced is thus twice the number of oxygen molecules. Assuming equal temperature and pressure for both gases, the produced hydrogen gas has therefore twice the volume of the produced oxygen gas. The number of electrons pushed through the water is twice the number of generated hydrogen molecules and four times the number of generated oxygen molecules.

Thermodynamics of the Process

Decomposition of pure water into hydrogen and oxygen at standard temperature and pressure is not favourable in thermodynamical terms. This is because, E (cell) = E (Oxidation) + E (Reduction). If E (cell) < 0, reaction is not favorable.

Anode (oxidation):

$$2H_2O\,(l) \rightarrow O_2(g) + 4H^+(aq) + 4e^- E^0_{0X} = -123V$$

Cathode (reduction):

$$2H^+(aq) + 2e^- \rightarrow H_2(g) \quad E^0_{red} = 0.00V$$

Thus, the standard potential of the water electrolysis cell is -1.23 V at 25 °C from the Nernst Equation.

The negative voltage indicates the Gibbs free energy for electrolysis of water is greater than zero for these reactions. This can be found using the G=-nFE equation from chemical kinetics, where n is the moles of electrons and F is the Faraday constant. The reaction cannot occur without adding necessary energy, usually supplied by an external electrical power source.

Electrolyte Selection

If the above described processes occur in pure water, H^+ cations will accumulate at the anode and OH^- anions will accumulate at the cathode. This can be verified by adding a pH indicator to the water: the water near the anode is acidic while the water near the cathode is basic. These charged ions will repel the further flow of electricity until they have diffused away, a slow process. This is why pure water conducts electricity poorly and why electrolysis of pure water proceeds slowly.

If a water-soluble electrolyte is added, the conductivity of the water rises considerably. The electrolyte disassociates into cations and anions; the anions rush towards the anode and neutralize the buildup of positively charged H^+ there; similarly, the cations rush towards the cathode and neutralize the buildup of negatively charged OH^- there. This allows the continued flow of electricity.

Care must be taken in choosing an electrolyte, since an anion from the electrolyte is in competition with the hydroxide ions to give up an electron. An electrolyte anion with less standard electrode potential than hydroxide will be oxidized instead of the hydroxide, and no oxygen gas will be produced. A cation with a greater standard electrode potential than a hydrogen ion will be reduced in its stead, and no hydrogen gas will be produced.

The following cations have lower electrode potential than H^+ and are therefore suitable for use as electrolyte cations: Li^+, Rb^+, K^+, Cs^+, Ba^{2+}, Sr^{2+}, Ca^{2+}, Na^+, and Mg^{2+}. Sodium and lithium are frequently used, as they form inexpensive, soluble salts.

If an acid is used as the electrolyte, the cation is H^+, and there is no competitor for the H^+ created by disassociating water. The most commonly used anion is sulfate (SO_4^{2-}), as it is very difficult to oxidize, with the standard potential for oxidation of this ion to the peroxodisulfate ion being -0.22 volts.

Strong acids such as sulfuric acid (H_2SO_4), and strong bases such as potassium hydroxide (KOH), and sodium hydroxide (NaOH) are frequently used as electrolytes.

A solid polymer electrolyte can also be used such as NAFION and when applied with a special catalyst on each side of the membrane can efficiently split the water molecule with as little as 1.8 Volts.

Techniques

Fundamental Demonstration

Two leads, running from the terminals of a battery, are placed in a cup of water with a quantity of electrolyte (not

NaCl, anode creates chlorine gas) added to establish conductivity. Hydrogen and oxygen gases will stream from the oppositely charged electrode. Oxygen will collect at the anode and hydrogen will collect at the cathode.

Hofmann Voltameter

The Hofmann voltameter is often used as a small-scale electrolytic cell. It consists of three joined upright cylinders. The inner cylinder is open at the top to allow the addition of water and the electrolyte. A platinum electrode is placed at the bottom of each of the two side cylinders, connected to the positive and negative terminals of a source of electricity. When current is run through the Hofmann voltameter, gaseous oxygen forms at the anode and gaseous hydrogen at the cathode. Each gas displaces water and collects at the top of the two outer tubes, where it can be drawn off with a stopcock.

Industrial Electrolysis

Many industrial electrolysis cells are very similar to Hofmann voltameters, with complex platinum plates or honeycombs as electrodes. Generally the only time hydrogen is intentionally produced from electrolysis is for specific point of use application such as is the case with oxyhydrogen torches or when extremely high hydrogen purity or oxygen is desired. The vast majority of hydrogen is produced from hydrocarbons and as a result contains trace amounts of carbon monoxide among other impurities. The carbon monoxide impurity can be detrimental to various systems including many fuel cells.

High Pressure Electrolysis

High pressure electrolysis is the electrolysis of water with a compressed hydrogen output around 120-200 Bar (1740-2900 psi). By pressurising the hydrogen in the electrolyser the need for an external hydrogen compressor is eliminated, the average energy consumption for internal compression is around three per cent.

Applications

About four percent of hydrogen gas produced worldwide is created by electrolysis. The majority of this hydrogen produced through electrolysis is a side product in the production of chlorine.

$$2\ NaCl + 2\ H_2O \rightarrow Cl_2 + H_2 + 2\ NaOH$$

The electrolysis of brine, a water sodium chloride mixture, is only half the electrolysis of water since the chloride ions are oxidized to chlorine rather than water being oxidized to oxygen. The hydrogen produced from this process is either burned, used for the production of specialty chemicals, or various other small scale applications.

The majority of hydrogen used industrially is derived from fossil fuels. One example is fossil fuel derived hydrogen used for the creation of ammonia for fertilizer via the Haber process and for converting heavy petroleum sources to lighter fractions via hydrocracking. The production of this hydrogen usually involves the formation of synthesis gas a mixture of H_2 and CO. Synthesis gas can be hydrogen enriched through the water gas shift reaction. In this reaction the carbon monoxide is reacted with water to produce more H_2 with CO_2 by-product.

Efficiency

Water electrolysis does not convert 100% of the electrical energy into the chemical energy of hydrogen. The process requires more extreme potentials than what would be expected based on the cell's total reversible reduction potentials. This excess potential accounts for various forms of over potential by which the extra energy is eventually lost as heat. For a well designed cell the largest over potential is the reaction over potential for the four electron oxidation of water to oxygen at the anode. An effective electrocatalyst to facilitate this reaction has not been developed. Platinum alloys are the default state of the art for this oxidation. The reverse reaction, the reduction of oxygen to water, is responsible for the greatest loss of efficiency in fuel cells. Developing a cheap effective electrocatalyst for this reaction would be a great advance.

The simpler two-electron reaction to produce hydrogen at the cathode can be electrocatalyzed with almost no reaction over potential by platinum or in theory a hydrogenase enzyme. If other, less effective, materials are used for the cathode then another large over potential must be paid.

The energy efficiency of water electrolysis varies widely with the numbers cited below on the optimistic side. Some report 50-80% These values refer only to the efficiency of converting electrical energy into hydrogen's chemical energy. The energy lost in generating the electricity is not included. For instance, when considering a power plant that converts the heat of nuclear reactions into hydrogen via electrolysis, the total efficiency may be closer to 30-45%.

CHEMICAL PROPERTIES OF WATER

Water is a special chemical substance consisting of two atoms of hydrogen and one atom of oxygen.

O—H bond length = 95.7 picometers

H—O—H angle = 104.5°

O-H bond energy = 450 kJ/mol

Dipole moment = 1.83 debyes

The hydrogen atoms are "attached" to one side of the oxygen atom, resulting in a water molecule having a positive charge on the side where the hydrogen atoms are and a negative charge on the other side, where the oxygen atom is.

Since opposite electrical charges attract, water molecules tend to attract each other, making water kind of "sticky."

The side with the hydrogen atoms (positive charge) attracts the oxygen side (negative charge) of a different water molecule.

The water molecule maintains a bent shape because of two considerations:

1. The tetrahedral arrangement around the oxygen.
2. The presence of lone pair electrons on the oxygen.

Two electrons not involved in the covalent bonds are called lone pair electrons. The pairs of electrons are left alone.

These lone pairs are very negative - containing two negative electrons each - and want to stay away from each other as much as possible. These repulsive forces act to push the hydrogens closer together. The net result is a terahedral arrangement.

Tetrahedral means "four-sided". It is the arrangement of four atoms around a central atom such that the distance between them is maximized.

The arrangement adopted will be the form of a regular tetrahedron. It has regular bond angles of 109.5°.

If we do a similar arrangement of water, putting oxygen in the center, and using the two hydrogens and two lone pairs at the corners, we also come up with a tetrahedral arrangement.

However, there is one important difference - the bond angles for water are not 109.5°. Because of the presence of the very negative lone pair electrons the two hydrogens are squeezed together as the two lone pairs try to get away from each other as far as possible. The resulting angle gives water a 104.5 bond angle.

Links Between Chemical Structure and Physical Properties

Two other features of the water molecule are also important for its properties:

- the small size of molecule; and
- the molecule is strongly dipolar.

This property makes water an effective solvent, particularly for crystalline salts. The small size of hydrogen atoms makes it possible for molecules of water to effectively bond together or chemically associate, particularly at lower temperatures. This gives water its surface tension and liquid properties and also gives water it's unique physical properties. However, water also partially dissociates into very minute concentrations of acid [H_3O^+] and base [OH^-] ions, a characteristic which leads to the use of the pH scale to measure relative acidity or alkalinity. This also helps in dissolving ions and transporting H^+ ions.

Major Chemical Properties of Water

Polarity

Two atoms, connected by a covalent bond, may exert different attractions for the electrons of the bond. In such cases the bond is polar, with one end slightly negatively charged (-) and the other slightly positively charged (+).

Although a water molecule has an overall neutral charge (having the same number of electrons and protons), the electrons are asymmetrically distributed, which makes the molecule polar. The oxygen nucleus draws electrons away from the hydrogen nuclei, leaving these nuclei with a small net positive charge. The excess of electron density on the oxygen atom creates weakly negative regions at the other two corners of an imaginary tetrahedron.

Water Structure - Hydrogen Bonds

Because they are polarized, two adjacent H_2O molecules can form a linkage known as a hydrogen bond. Hydrogen bonds have only about 1/20 the strength of a covalent bond. A hydrogen bond is therefore a weak chemical bond between a hydrogen atom in one polar molecule and a very electronegative atom of a second polar molecule. The hydrogen of one water molecule will be attracted to the oxygen of another water molecule. The are usually 4-8 molecules per group in liquid water. The surface tension of water is due to the hydrogen bonding in the associated groups of water molecules.

Hydrogen bonds are strongest when the three atoms lie in a straight line. The cohesive nature of water, through the hydrogen bonding and the small size of the molecule, allowing the molecules to pack together, is responsible for many of its unusual properties, such as high surface tension, specific heat, and heat of vapourization. Molecules of water join together transiently in a hydrogen-bonded lattice. Even at 37 °C, 15% of the water molecules are joined to four others in a short-lived assembly known as a "flickering cluster."

Hydrophylic ('Water Loving') and Hydrophobic ('Water Hating') Molecules

Hydrophylic Molecules

Substances that dissolve readily in water are termed hydrophilic. They are composed of ions or polar molecules that attract water molecules through electrical charge effects. Water molecules surround each ion or polar molecule on the surface of a solid substance and carry it into solution. Ionic substances such as sodium chloride dissolve because water molecules are attracted to the positive (Na^+) or negative (Cl^-) charge of each ion. Polar substances such as urea dissolve because their molecules form hydrogen bonds with the surrounding water molecules.

Hydrophobic Molecules

Molecules that contain a preponderance of nonpolar bonds are usually insoluble in water and are termed 'hydrophobic'. This is true, especially, of hydrocarbons, which contain many C-H bonds. Water molecules are not attracted to such molecules as much as they are to other water molecules and so have little tendency to surround them and carry them into solution.

But the so-called 'Hydrophobic Effect' does not mean that nonpolar molecules are not attracted to water! We have all seen what happens after vinegar and oil salad dressing are vigorously shaken; one does get a mixture of sorts, but after a little time the ingredients separate with the lighter oil on top and a denser vinegar/water solution on bottom. This is an illustration of an important chemistry principle expressed by the rule that 'like dissolves like.' This refers to the phenomena that when two liquids made of molecules of similar size and polarities are mixed, they will usually form a single phase solution, no matter what the relative number of moles of each species. This is expressed by the jargon that the two substances are miscible in all proportions.

In contrast, when a highly polar substance, such as water, is mixed with a nonpolar or weakly polar substance, such as most oils, the substances will separate into two phases. This phenomenon is usually rationalized in introductory chemistry text books by saying that oil is hydrophobic, and thus does not make solutions with water, while polar small organic acids (such as acetic acid from which house vinegar is made) are hydrophilic, and thus are miscible with water.

This explanation almost universally leads people to believe that individual water and oil repel each other, or at least attract each other very weakly. Nothing can be further from the case! An individual oil molecule is attracted to a water molecule by a force that is much greater than the attraction of two oil molecules to each other. We can observe the consequence of this greater attraction when we put a drop of oil on a clean surface of water. Before hitting the surface, the oil will be in the shape of a spherical droplet.

This is because the oil molecules are attracted to one another and a spherical shape minimizes the number of oil molecules that are not surrounded by other molecules. When the oil hits the surface of the water, it spreads out to form a thin layer. This happens because the attractions between the oil and water molecules gained by spreading over the surface is larger than the oil-oil attraction lost in making a large oil surface on top of the water. If a sufficiently small drop of oil is put on the surface, it will spread to form a single molecular layer of oil.

By measuring the area produced, one can get a simple estimate for the size of each oil molecule and thus Avogadro's number. Given these strong interactions, why does not each oil molecule dive into the water solution? And surround itself with the favorable water attractions? The reason is that to do so, it must come between water molecules that are already attracting each other! The strength of water-water attraction is much higher than water-oil interactions, and thus there is a net cost of energy in putting the oil molecules into a water solution. Thus the vast majority of oil molecules stay out of the water, though as many as will fit will hang on to the surface water molecules that do not have a full complement of partners. The meniscus is the curved surface of a liquid in a graduated cylinder or any other small diameter glassware. Water adheres to the sides of any container creating a "cup" of surface tension.

This induced structure is very important is it related to the structure and function of membranes which are very characteristic of life as we know it. Membranes in bacteria are composed of phospholipids and proteins. Phospholipids contain a charged or polar group (often phosphate, hence the name) attached to a 3 carbon glycerol back bone. There are also two fatty acid chains dangling from the other carbons of glycerol. The phosphate end of the molecule is hydrophilic and is attracted to water. The fatty acids are hydrophobic and are driven away from water.

Because phospholipids have hydrophobic and hydrophilic portions, they do remarkable things. When placed in an aqueous environment, the hydrophobic portions stick together, as do the hydrophilic. A very stable form of this arrangement is the lipid bilayer. This way the hydrophobic parts of the molecule form one layer, as do the hydrophilic. Lipid bilayers form spontaneously if phospholipids are placed in an aqueous environment. The cytoplasmic membrane is stabilized by hydrophobic interactions (i.e. water induced) between neighboring lipids and by hydrogen bonds between neighboring lipids. Hydrogen bonds can also form between membrane proteins and lipids. These are known as membrane vesicles and are used to study membrane properties experimentally. There is some evidence that these structures may form abiotically and may occur on particles that rain down on earth from space.

Water as a Solvent - Acids & Bases - pH - Hydration

Water as a Solvent

Many substances, such as household sugar, dissolve in water. That is, their molecules separate from each other, each becoming surrounded by water molecules. When a substance dissolves in a liquid, the mixture is termed a solution. The dissolved substance (in this case sugar) is the solute, and the liquid that does the dissolving (in this case water) is the solvent. Water is an excellent solvent for many substances because of its polar bonds.

Acids

Substances that release hydrogen ions into solution are called acids. Many of the acids important in the cell are only partially dissociated, and they are therefore weak acids-for example, the carboxyl group (-COOH), which dissociates to give a hydrogen ion in solution. Note that this is a reversible reaction.

Bases

Substances that reduce the number of hydrogen ions in solution are called bases. Some bases, such as ammonia, combine directly with hydrogen ions. Other bases, such as sodium hydroxide, reduce the number of H^+ ions indirectly, by making OH- ions that then combine directly with H^+ ions to make H_2O. Many bases found in cells are partially dissociated and are termed weak bases. This is true of compounds that contain an amino group ($-NH_2$), which has a weak tendency to reversibly accept an H^+ ion from water, increasing the quantity of free OH^- ions.

Hydrogen Ion Exchange

Positively charged hydrogen ions (H^+) can spontaneously move from one water molecule to another, thereby creating two ionic species. Since the process is rapidly reversible, hydrogen ions are continually shuttling between water molecules. Pure water contains a steady state concentration of hydrogen ions and hydroxyl ions (both 10^{-7} M).

pH

The acidity of a solution is defined by the concentration of H^+ ions it possesses. For convenience we use the pH scale, where pH = _log10[H^+].

For pure water [H^+] = 10^{-7} moles/litre.

Links Between Chemical Structure and Physical Properties

Water (H_2O) is a very unusual substance with many strange and unique properties that are so important to Life on Planet Water - Life which is based on Water and adapted to its unique and anomalous properties. How does this simple molecule, composed of two hydrogen atoms and one oxygen atom, behave the way it does and how does it support life? Some familiar properties of water are:

- It's colourless;
- It's tasteless;
- It's odourless;
- It feels wet;
- It dissolves nearly everything;
- It exists in three forms: liquid, solid, gas, and is cycled though the water cycle;
- It can absorb a large amount of heat; It sticks together into beads or drops;
- It flows and erodes the surface of the earth; it moves sediments to form beaches, river banks and bars;
- It shapes lipid and protein molecules and give them their 3-dimensional form which is critical to their function; and
- It's part of every living organism on the planet.

Many of water's unique properties are largely a result of its chemical structure. The two hydrogen atoms bound to one oxygen atom to form a 'V' shape with the hydrogen atoms at an angle of 105°. When the hydrogen atoms combine with oxygen, they each give away their single electron and form a covalent bond. Because electrons are more attracted to the positively charged oxygen atom, the two hydrogens become slightly positively charged (they give away their negative charge) and the oxygen atom becomes negatively charged. This separation between negative and positive charges produces a polar molecule, that is a molecule that has an electrical charge on its surface. The hydrogen lobes have positive charges, and the oxygen atom on the opposite side has two negative charges associated with two lobes. The net interaction between the covalent bond and the attracting and repulsion between the positive and negative charges repelling charges produces the 'V' shape of the molecule.

The polarity of water allows it to bind with other molecules, including itself. The water molecules form hydrogen bonds, giving shape to water as a liquid. Each single water molecule can form bonds with four other water molecules in a tetrahedral arrangement. Although these bonds are weak they lead to many other unique properties. The V-shape of the water molecule is also important because it allows for other configurations of water to be formed. Ice, for instance, has a very ordered lattice structure. Super cooled water (water below the freezing point) also has water molecules that are structured in a certain way. Snowflakes have yet another shape.

Physical Properties and Life

Life on Planet Water depends on the unique and unusual properties of water. Water is 'mother' and 'matrix' for life.

- The large heat capacity and high water content in organisms contribute to thermal regulation and prevent local temperature fluctuations.
- The high latent heat of evaporation gives resistance to dehydration and considerable evaporative cooling.
- Water is an excellent solvent due to its polarity, high dielectric constant and small size, particularly for polar and ionic compounds and salts.
- It has unique hydration properties towards biological molecules (particularly lipids, proteins and nucleic acids) that determine their three-dimensional structures, and hence their functions, in solution. This hydration forms gels that can reversibly undergo the gel-sol phase transitions that underlie many cellular mechanisms.
- Water ionizes and allows easy proton exchange between molecules, so contributing to the richness of the ionic interactions in biology.

- The density maximum at 4 °C and low ice density means that all of a body of water (not just its surface) is close to 0 °C before any freezing can occur. Also the freezing of rivers, lakes and oceans is from the top down, so insulating the water from further freezing and allowing rapid thawing, and density driven thermal convection causing seasonal mixing in deeper temperate waters.
- The large heat capacity of the oceans and seas allows them to act as heat reservoirs such that sea temperatures vary only a third as much as land temperatures and so moderate our climate.
- The compressibility of water reduces the sea level by about 40 m giving us 5% more land.

Hydrophylic ('Water Loving') and Hydrophobic ('Water Hating') Molecules

Hydrophylic Molecules

Substances that dissolve readily in water are termed 'hydrophilic'. They are composed of ions or polar molecules that attract water molecules through electrical charge effects. Water molecules surround each ion or polar molecule on the surface of a solid substance and carry it into solution. Ionic substances such as sodium chloride dissolve because water molecules are attracted to the positive (Na^+) or negative (Cl^-) charge of each ion. Polar substances such as urea dissolve because their molecules form hydrogen bonds with the surrounding water molecules.

Hydrophobic Molecules

Molecules that contain mostly nonpolar bonds are usually insoluble in water and are termed 'hydrophobic'. This is true, especially, of hydrocarbons, which contain many C-H bonds. Water molecules are less attracted to such molecules than they are to other water molecules and so have little tendency to surround them and carry them into solution. But the so-called 'Hydrophobic Effect' does not mean that nonpolar molecules are not attracted to water! When a highly polar substance, such as water, is mixed with a nonpolar or weakly polar substance, such as most oils, the substances will separate into two phases.

This phenomenon is usually rationalized in introductory chemistry text books by saying that oil is hydrophobic. Most people wrongly believe that this means that individual water and oil molecules repel each other, or at least attract each other very weakly. However, this is clearly wrong and misleading! In face an individual oil molecule is attracted to a water molecule by a force that is much greater than the attraction of two oil molecules to each other. This can be demonstrated when a drop of oil is placed onto a clean surface of water. Originally the oil will be in the shape of a spherical droplet, because the oil molecules are attracted to one another and a spherical shape minimizes the number of oil molecules that are not surrounded by other molecules.

When the oil droplet hits the surface of the water, it spreads out to form a thin layer. This happens because the oil and water bonds formed by the oil forming a layer on the surface of the water are stronger than the oil-oil attraction in the oil droplet. If a sufficiently small drop of oil is put on the surface, it will spread to form a single molecular layer of oil.

Given these strong interactions, why doesn't each oil molecule dive into the water solution? And become completely surrounded with water molecules? The reason is that the water-water bonds are much stronger! Displacing the water molecules would cost more energy. Consequently most of the oil molecules stay out of the water, though as many as will fit will hang on to the surface water molecules that do not have a full complement of partners. A similar explanation applies for the meniscus, that is the curved surface of a liquid in a graduated cylinder or any other small diameter glassware. Water adheres to the sides of any container creating a "cup" of surface tension. The induced structure produced through the interaction with water molecules is very important as it is related to the structure and function of membranes which are very characteristic of life as we know it. Membranes in bacteria are composed of phospholipids and proteins.

Phospholipids contain a charged or polar group (often phosphate, hence the name) attached to a 3 carbon glycerol back bone. There are also two fatty acid chains dangling from the other carbons of glycerol. The phosphate end of the molecule is hydrophilic and is attracted to water. The fatty acids are hydrophobic and are driven away from water. Because phospholipids have hydrophobic and hydrophilic portions, they do remarkable things. When placed in an aqueous environment, the hydrophobic portions stick together, as do the hydrophilic bits. A very stable form of this arrangement is the lipid bilayer.

This way the hydrophobic parts of the molecule form one layer, as do the hydrophilic. Lipid bilayers form spontaneously if phospholipids are placed in an aqueous environment. The cytoplasmic membrane is stabilized by hydrophobic interactions (i.e. water induced) between neighboring lipids and by hydrogen bonds between neighboring lipids. Hydrogen bonds can also form between membrane proteins and lipids. These are known as membrane vesicles and are used to study membrane properties experimentally. There is some evidence that these structures may form abiotically and may occur on particles that rain down on earth from space.

Extract Air to make Oil and Water Mix

One of the great truths of life, that oil and water do not mix, has been turned on its head. The secret to making them mix without chemicals, according to Ric Pashley, a chemist at Canberra's Australian National University, is extracting all the dissolved air from the water. "It makes an emulsion, not quite as cloudy as milk," the chemist said. The discovery, which could lead to everything from new medicines to paints and perfumes, has delighted scientists around the world.

In 1982, Professor Pashley discovered something called long-range hydrophobic force, now accepted as the reason oil and water do not normally mix. He explained that oil droplets can attract each other over a distance as large as their own radius. As a result, oil droplets merge rather than disperse in water.

A typical litre of water, he noted, contains about two milliliters of dissolved air. Suspecting that was the problem, he extracted 99.999 per cent of the dissolved air from some water. To his joy, it mixed with oil, forming an emulsion that did not separate. Water as a Solvent - Acids & Bases - pH - Hydration.

9 Water Pollution

Water pollution is the contamination of water bodies such as lakes, rivers, oceans, and groundwater caused by human activities, which can be harmful to organisms and plants that live in these water bodies.

Water pollution is a major problem in the global context. It has been suggested that it is the leading worldwide cause of deaths and diseases and that it accounts for the deaths of more than 14,000 people daily. In addition to the acute problems of water pollution in developing countries, industrialized countries continue to struggle with pollution problems as well. In the most recent national report on water quality in the United States, 45 per cent of assessed stream miles, 47 per cent of assessed lake acres, and 32 per cent of assessed bay and estuarine square miles were classified as polluted.

Water is typically referred to as polluted when it is impaired by anthropogenic contaminants and either does not support a human use, like serving as drinking water, and/ or undergoes a marked shift in its ability to support its constituent biotic communities, such as fish. Natural phenomena such as volcanoes, algae blooms, storms, and earthquakes also cause major changes in water quality and the ecological status of water. Water pollution has many causes and characteristics.

Water Pollution Categories

Surface water and groundwater have often been studied and managed as separate resources, although they are interrelated. Sources of surface water pollution are generally grouped into two categories based on their origin.

Point Source Pollution

Point source pollution refers to contaminants that enter a waterway through a discrete conveyance, such as a pipe or ditch. Examples of sources in this category include discharges from a sewage treatment plant, a factory, or a city storm drain. The U.S. Clean Water Act (CWA) defines point source for regulatory enforcement purposes.

Non-point Source Pollution

Non-point source (NPS) pollution refers to diffuse contamination that does not originate from a single discrete source. NPS pollution is often a cumulative effect of small amounts of contaminants gathered from a large area. Nutrient runoff in stormwater from "sheet flow" over an agricultural field or a forest are sometimes cited as examples of NPS pollution.

Contaminated stormwater washed off of parking lots, roads and highways, called urban runoff, is sometimes included under the category of NPS pollution. However, this runoff is typically channeled into storm drain systems and discharged through pipes to local surface waters, and is a point source. The CWA definition of point source was amended in 1987 to include municipal storm sewer systems, as well as industrial stormwater, such as from construction sites.

Groundwater Pollution

Interactions between groundwater and surface water are complex. Consequently, groundwater pollution, sometimes referred to as groundwater contamination, is not as easily classified as surface water pollution By its very nature, groundwater aquifers are susceptible to contamination from sources that may not directly affect surface water bodies, and the distinction of point vs. non-point source may be irrelevant. A spill of a chemical contaminant on soil, located away from a surface water body, may not necessarily create point source or non-point source pollution, but nonetheless may contaminate the aquifer below. Analysis of groundwater contamination may focus on soil characteristics and hydrology, as well as the nature of the contaminant itself.

Materials and Phenomena Contributing to Water Pollution

The specific contaminants leading to pollution in water include a wide spectrum of chemicals, pathogens, and physical or sensory changes such as elevated temperature and discoloration. While many of the chemicals and substances that are regulated may be naturally occurring (calcium, sodium, iron, manganese, etc.) the concentration is often the key in determining what is a natural component of water, and what is a contaminant.

Oxygen-depleting substances may be natural materials, such as plant matter (e.g. leaves and grass) as well as man-made chemicals. Other natural and anthropogenic substances may cause turbidity (cloudiness) which blocks light and disrupts plant growth, and clogs the gills of some fish species.

Many of the chemical substances are toxic. Pathogens can produce waterborne diseases in either human or animal hosts. Alteration of water's physical chemistry include acidity (change in pH), electrical conductivity, temperature, and eutrophication. Eutrophication is the fertilization of surface water by nutrients that were previously scarce.

Pathogens

Coliform bacteria are a commonly-used bacterial indicator of water pollution, although not an actual cause of disease. Other microorganisms sometimes found in surface waters which have caused human health problems include:

- *Cryptosporidium parvum*
- *Giardia lamblia*
- Salmonella
- High levels of pathogens may result from inadequately treated sewage discharges or livestock operations.
- Chemical and other contaminants
- Contaminants may include organic and inorganic substances.

Organic water pollutants include:

- Detergents
- Disinfection by-products found in chemically disinfected drinking water, such as chloroform
- Food processing waste, which can include oxygen-demanding substances, fats and grease.
- Insecticides and herbicides, a huge range of organohalides and other chemical compounds.
- Petroleum hydrocarbons, including fuels (gasoline, diesel fuel, jet fuels, and fuel oil) and lubricants (motor oil), and fuel combustion by-products, from stormwater runoff.

Tree and brush debris from logging operations.

Volatile organic compounds (VOCs), such as industrial solvents, from improper storage. Chlorinated solvents, which are dense non-aqueous phase liquids (DNAPLs), may fall to the bottom of reservoirs, since they don't mix well with water and are denser.

Various chemical compounds found in personal hygiene and cosmetic products.

Inorganic water pollutants include:

- Acidity caused by industrial discharges (especially sulfur dioxide from power plants).
- Ammonia from food processing waste.
- Chemical waste as industrial by-products.

Fertilizers containing nutrients—nitrates and phosphates—which are found in stormwater runoff from agriculture, as well as commercial and residential use.

Heavy metals from motor vehicles (via urban stormwater runoff and acid mine drainage.

Silt (sediment) in runoff from construction sites, logging, slash and burn practices or land clearing sites.

Macroscopic pollution—large visible items polluting the water—may be termed "floatables" in an urban stormwater context, or marine debris when found on the open seas, and can include such items as:

- Trash (e.g. paper, plastic, or food waste) discarded by people on the ground, and that are washed by rainfall into storm drains and eventually discharged into surface waters.
- Nurdles, small ubiquitous waterborne plastic pellets.
- Shipwrecks, large derelict ships.
- Transport and chemical reactions of water pollutants.

Environment Portal

Most water pollutants are eventually carried by rivers into the oceans. In some areas of the world the influence can be traced hundred miles from the mouth by studies using hydrology transport models. Advanced computer models such as SWMM or the DSSAM Model have been used in many locations worldwide to examine the fate of pollutants in aquatic systems. Indicator filter feeding species such as copepods have also been used to study pollutant fates in the New York Bight, for example. The highest toxin loads are not directly at the mouth of the Hudson River, but 100 kilometers south, since several days are required for incorporation into planktonic tissue. The Hudson discharge flows south along the coast due to coriolis force. Further south then are areas of oxygen depletion, caused by chemicals using up oxygen and by algae blooms, caused by excess nutrients from algal cell death and decomposition. Fish and shellfish kills have been reported, because toxins climb the food chain after small fish consume copepods, then large fish eat smaller fish, etc. Each successive step up the food chain causes a stepwise concentration of pollutants such as heavy metals (e.g. mercury) and persistent organic pollutants such as DDT. This is known as biomagnification, which is occasionally used interchangeably with bioaccumulation.

Large gyres (vortexes) in the oceans trap floating plastic debris. The North Pacific Gyre for example has collected the so-called "Great Pacific Garbage Patch" that is now estimated at 100 times the size of Texas. Many of these long-lasting pieces wind up in the stomachs of marine birds and animals. This results in obstruction of digestive pathways which leads to reduced appetite or even starvation.

Many chemicals undergo reactive decay or chemically change especially over long periods of time in groundwater reservoirs. A noteworthy class of such chemicals is the chlorinated hydrocarbons such as trichloroethylene (used in industrial metal degreasing and electronics manufacturing) and tetrachloroethylene used in the dry cleaning industry (note latest advances in liquid carbon dioxide in dry cleaning that avoids all use of chemicals). Both of these chemicals, which are carcinogens themselves, undergo partial decomposition reactions, leading to new hazardous chemicals (including dichloroethylene and vinyl chloride).

Groundwater pollution is much more difficult to abate than surface pollution because groundwater can move great distances through unseen aquifers. Non-porous aquifers such as clays partially purify water of bacteria by simple filtration (adsorption and absorption), dilution, and, in some cases, chemical reactions and biological activity: however, in some cases, the pollutants merely transform to soil contaminants. Groundwater that moves through cracks and caverns is not filtered and can be transported as easily as surface water. In fact, this can be aggravated by the human tendency to use natural sinkholes as dumps in areas of Karst topography.

There are a variety of secondary effects stemming not from the original pollutant, but a derivative condition. Some of these secondary impacts are:

- Silt-bearing surface runoff from can inhibit the penetration of sunlight through the water column, hampering photosynthesis in aquatic plants.
- Thermal pollution can induce fish kills and invasion by new thermophilic species. This can cause further problems to existing wildlife.

Measurement of Water Pollution

Water pollution may be analyzed through several broad categories of methods: physical, chemical and biological. Most methods involve collection of samples, followed by specialized analytical tests. Some methods may be conducted in situ, without sampling, such as temperature. Government agencies and research organizations have published standardized, validated analytical test methods to facilitate the comparability of results from disparate testing events.

Sampling

Sampling of water for physical or chemical testing can be done by several methods, depending on the accuracy needed and the characteristics of the contaminant. Many contamination events are sharply restricted in time, most commonly in association with rain events. For this reason "grab" samples are often inadequate for fully quantifying contaminant levels. Scientists gathering this type of data often employ auto-sampler devices that pump increments of water at either time or discharge intervals.

Sampling for biological testing involves collection of plants and/or animals from the surface water body. Depending on the type of assessment, the organisms may be identified for biosurveys (population counts) and returned to the water body, or they may be dissected for bioassays to determine toxicity.

Physical Testing

Common physical tests of water include temperature, solids concentration and turbidity.

Chemical Testing

Water samples may be examined using the principles of analytical chemistry. Many published test methods are available for both organic and inorganic compounds. Frequently-used methods include pH, biochemical oxygen demand (BOD), chemical oxygen demand (COD), nutrients (nitrate and phosphorus compounds), metals (including copper, zinc, cadmium, lead and mercury), oil and grease, total petroleum hydrocarbons (TPH), and pesticides.

Biological Testing

Biological testing involves the use of plant, animal, and/or microbial indicators to monitor the health of an aquatic ecosystem.

Control of Water Pollution

Domestic Sewage

In urban areas, domestic sewage is typically treated by centralized sewage treatment plants. In the U.S., most of these plants are operated by local government agencies. Municipal treatment plants are designed to control conventional pollutants: BOD and suspended solids. Well-designed and operated systems can remove 90 percent or more of these pollutants. Some plants have additional sub-systems to treat nutrients and pathogens. Most municipal plants are not designed to treat toxic pollutants found in industrial wastewater.

A household or business not served by a municipal treatment plant may have an individual septic tank, which treats the wastewater on site and discharges into the soil. Alternatively, domestic wastewater may be sent to a nearby privately-owned treatment system (e.g. in a rural community).

Industrial Wastewater

Some industrial facilities generate ordinary domestic sewage that can be treated by municipal facilities. Industries that generate wastewater with high concentrations of conventional pollutants (e.g oil and grease), toxic pollutants (e.g. heavy metals, volatile organic compounds) or other non-conventional pollutants such as ammonia, need specialized treatment systems. Some of these facilities can install a pre-treatment system to remove the toxic components, and then send the partially-treated wastewater to the municipal system. Industries generating large volumes of wastewater typically operate their own complete on-site treatment systems.

Some industries have been successful at redesigning their manufacturing processes to reduce or eliminate pollutants, through a process called pollution prevention.

Construction Site Stormwater

Sediment (loose soil) from construction sites is managed by installation of:

- erosion controls, such as mulching; and
- sediment controls, such as sediment basins and silt fences.

Discharge of toxic chemicals such as motor fuels and concrete washout is prevented by use of:

- spill prevention and control plans; and
- specially-designed containers (e.g. for concrete washout) and structures such as overflow controls and diversion berms.

Urban Runoff (Stormwater)

Effective control of urban runoff involves reducing the velocity and flow of stormwater, as well as reducing pollutant discharges. Local governments use a variety of stormwater management techniques to reduce the effects of urban runoff. These techniques, called best management practices (BMPs) in the U.S., may focus on water quantity control, while others focus on improving water quality, and some perform both functions.

Light in Water

The Earth is often referred to as the 'Water Planet' or 'Planet Ocean.'

It is undeniable that no matter who we are where we live or eventually how we will make a living, the oceans touch all of our lives. It sustains us and provides us nourishment.

Water covers over seventy percent (70%) of our planet. The ocean supports an abundance of life and provides more than seventy percent of the Earth's oxygen. How is this possible? Through a series of classroom activities, students will examine the physics of light absorption in water to gain a better understanding of Earth's dependency on sunlight for essential life-sustaining processes as photosynthesis and how it affects interdependent biota as well as how the light spectrum is affected by depth in aquatic systems.

Students will learn and be introduced to key vocabulary terms during the course of this unit that will enhance their comprehension of the subject: Amplitude, Biota/Biomass, Frequency, Solar Energy, Photon, Photosynthesis, Nanometer and Wavelength. During the class discussions, students will learn and investigate that white light encompasses the full spectrum of colors in the rainbow with each color assigned a varying wavelength. In addition, students will discover the specific wavelengths of basic colors - Red, Orange, Yellow, Green, Blue and Violet; understand that colors are absorbed at different depths as well as see the correlation that photosynthesis takes place at certain wavelengths of light.

Educators will need to refresh their knowledge on some pertinent background information before presenting this lesson to their students. Water absorbs light. The energy from the Sun or 'Solar Energy' is the primary source of light that is vital to both aquatic and terrestrial ecosystems. This white light that is transmitted by the Sun is necessary for plant growth which support the majority of living (Biotic) things that depend on plants either directly or indirectly for their food. The zone or depth at which light penetrates in water allowing plants to exist is known as the 'Photic Zone'. Water is transparent, meaning it allows light to pass through it. The amount of light that penetrates the water depends on its `turbidity' or the amount of dissolved minerals, silt and detritus material contained in it. These particles cause light in water to be scattered and absorbed rather than transmitted. As light penetrates this area, the colors are absorbed at different depths. This process of light absorption is based on wavelength, the shorter the wavelength of light, the greater the depth it penetrates. Therefore, red light is absorbed first by water and does not penetrate as far as the blue or violet light. The wavelengths of the various colors in the light spectrum are:

Colour	Wavelength
Red	780 to 622 nm
Orange	622 to 597 nm
Yellow	597 to 577 nm
Green	577 to 492 nm
Blue	492 to 455 nm
Violet	455 to 390 nm

Wavelengths of light are expressed in units of nanometers.

1 nm (nanometer) = 10^{-9} m

The nature of light behaves both as a wave phenomenon and as a particle of energy called 'photons'. If we examine light as a wave phenomenon, we can determine that it has a 'wavelength' (the distance from one peak of the wave to the next) and an 'amplitude' (the distance the wave oscillates or vibrates from its centerline). Light can also travel at various speeds in different media, producing a 'frequency' (the number of complete cycles of a wave that occur within a period of time) at which the wave travels. The energy contained in a wave of light is related to its frequency. Short wavelengths (colours such as blue and violet light) have high energies and long wavelengths have lower energies (colours such as red, orange, yellow and green). Hence, the colours of the spectrum with the longer wavelengths are not able to penetrate as deeply in water as the colours with the shorter wavelengths.

Within the photic zone, the colors of the light spectrum are able to penetrate through water before being absorbed at varying depths. The following data illustrate how the light spectrum is affected by depth:

Colour	Depth
Red	5 m
Orange	15 m
Yellow	30 m
Green	60 m
Blue	75 m
Indigo	85 m
Violet	100 m

Note: Depth is expressed in units of meters. Sea level was used as the point of origin for all recorded depth measurements.

The colour of our oceans and other large bodies of water depend on a number of variables, the two most important of which are the amount of ions and the amount of plant life in the water, namely phytoplankton (a microscopic plant that floats freely in the lighted surface waters). A body of water with a high concentration of plankton appears blue-green due to the presence of the green pigment chlorophyll. Very pure water appears deep blue, almost black and denotes the presence of very few ions and consequently little plant life.

Activities and Procedures

Light to Sea by (Activity 37): Addresses what happens to light when it moves through water? What happens to light in deep water?

This activity asks students questions about both changes in light intensity (quantity) and Quality (the color present) when light shines through water. The results are not clear-cut measurements, but value judgements (observations) made by students who may have different sensitivity to colors. The science skills used in this activity are observing, inferring and predicting. The concepts covered in this activity are water absorbs light, water absorbs different wavelengths at different rates and things like sediment suspended (turbidity) in the water absorb light.

This lesson will involve a teacher demonstration and a teacher directed group work activity (divide the class into groups of no more than four students). Different kind of introductions for this exercise are appropriate, depending on the background of your students (this lesson should build on prior knowledge). Have they ever looked at a spectrum? A rainbow? Do they understand that light bouncing off an object is reflected to their eyes? Do they know that the color of objects are determined by which colors (wavelengths) of light they reflect? Begin with a discussion of what your students know about light. Make sure they remember the difference between quantity or brightness (intensity) and Quality or colors of light.

How does water affect sunlight quantity and quality available to plants and animals. Living in water? Show the jars of clean and dirty water. Put white paper behind them. Tell the students you are going to shine a light through the jars. Ask the students to predict which transmitted light will be brighter: the light shining through the clear water or the dirty (Turbid) water? Which jar transmitted a greater quantity of light? Can they identify a natural event that would mimic the turbid jar?

Then demonstrate light quality. Use a prism and the slide projector or a beam of sunlight in a darkened room to show the colors that make up white light. Make your classroom as dark as possible so the students can see this clearly. What are the colors? What is their order in the spectrum? The order is in an increasing wavelength from blue (short) to green to yellow to orange to red (long). Have the students write the colors out in order as they observe them.

What happens if you put colored cellophane over the light source? (the end of the projector lens or the flashlight) before it reaches the prism? Try it with several layers of blue then red and green if you have them. The students should be able to see that parts of the spectrum are blocked by the transparent cellophane. It is absorbing some of the colors of light. The color transmitted is the color of the material. Put increasing number of layers of blue over the lens. Do not discuss this!

Then ask the group of students to address two questions. Does water absorb light, reducing the quantity of light in deeper water? Does water absorb some colors of light more than others? Give groups of student's pictures taken underwater under natural light (everything looks blue), close-ups with bright colors and pictures with a bright foreground and blue background. Can these differences in underwater pictures be explained? Let groups discuss their ideas for about 5-10 minutes. Have each group write its ideas and answers for the two questions (record in their science journals). Have the class discuss and clarify its ideas. Pass around one or more pictures of divers using a camera with a flash or other light source. Does this help explain what the students have observed in the set of pictures? Compare the blue pictures with what happened when you put blue cellophane over the light. Blue is transmitted and the other colors are absorbed in the same way that water absorbs some wavelengths and transmits blue.

A Light Snack (Activity 40): addresses the relationship between light availability and photosynthesis in aquatic plants. Student experiments measuring dissolved oxygen.

The science skills applied in this unit are measuring, organizing, inferring, predicting, experimenting and communicating. The concepts learned and discussed in this unit.

- If sufficient light is available, plants produce more oxygen in photosynthesis than they use in respiration.
- The amount of oxygen produced is proportional to the available light up to a point.

The mode of instruction for this unit is a teacher directed group work (Students remain in previously arranged groups of up to four students per group). The objective is for students to design and complete an experiment to test how the amount of light affects photosynthesis rates in aquatic plants. (Note: Both complete lessons along with a hard copy of my teaching unit will be mailed to you).

Assessment Strategies

The assessment of the student's knowledge of this unit is achieved by a three-fold method. First, the students will receive a quiz to test their knowledge and comprehension of the key vocabulary words. Second, the students will work in their cooperative work groups to complete the interactive lab exercise and class activities both of which will be recorded in their science journals and submitted for grading. Finally, upon completion of these two consecutive activities/ interactive lab students will demonstrate mastery of the concepts learned and discussed via an oral group presentation of their laboratory reports which includes a visual (ex. A graph, chart or an illustration of key concepts learned). An established rubric will be used for grading the group presentations and will be provided to the students.

Closure and Standards Addressed

Students to better understand the relationship between light absorption, photosynthesis, depth, temperature and nutrient load and its impacts on aquatic life and/or the productivity of lakes and oceans.

- Describe the nature of light as a wave phenomenon as it moves through an aquatic system, discuss how light is affected by water depth and how light transfers energy.
- Explain the ecological connections that are evident between solar energy and its impact on the hydrosphere, as it pertains to light absorption, photosynthesis and the interdependent biota.
- Learn, investigate and communicate their findings via a laboratory report, oral team presentation and appropriate visuals/models using appropriate technology, books, and reference materials as well as through reconstructing previously learned knowledge.

Proton Donors and Acceptors

The older Arrhenius theory of acids and bases viewed them as substances which produce hydrogen ions or hydroxide ions on dissociation. As useful a concept as this has been, it was unable to explain why NH_3, which contains no OH^- ions, is a base and not an acid, why a solution of $FeCl_3$ is acidic, or why a solution of Na_2S is alkaline.

A more general theory of acids and bases was developed by Franklin in 1905, who suggested that the solvent plays a central role. According to this view, an acid is a solute that gives rise to a cation (positive ion) characteristic of the solvent, and a base is a solute that yields a anion (negative ion) which is also characteristic of the solvent. The most important of these solvents is of course H_2O, but Franklin's insight extended the realm of acid-base chemistry into non-aqueous systems as we shall see in a later lesson.

Brønsted Acids and Bases

In 1923 the Danish chemist J.N. Brønsted, building on Franklin's theory, proposed that an acid is a proton donor; a base is a proton acceptor.

In the same year the English chemist T.M. Lowry published a paper setting forth some similar ideas without producing a definition; in a later paper Lowry himself points out that Brønsted deserves the major credit, but the concept is still widely known as the Brønsted-Lowry theory.

These definitions carry a very important implication: a substance cannot act as an acid without the presence of a base to accept the proton, and vice versa. As a very simple example, consider the equation that Arrhenius wrote to describe the behavior of hydrochloric acid:

$HCl \rightarrow H^+ + A^-$

This is fine as far as it goes, and chemists still write such an equation as a shortcut. But in order to represent this more realistically as a proton donor-acceptor reaction, we now depict the behavior of HCl in water by in which the acid HCl donates its proton to the acceptor (base) H_2O.

$HCl + H_2O \rightarrow Cl^- + H_3O^+$

acid base hydronium ion

"Nothing new here", you might say, noting that we are simply replacing a shorter equation by a longer one. But consider how we might explain the alkaline solution that is created when ammonia gas NH3 dissolves in water. An alkaline solution contains an excess of hydroxide ions, so ammonia is clearly a base, but because there are no OH– ions in NH3, it is clearly not an Arrhenius base. It is, however, a Brønsted base:

$NH_3 + H_2O \rightarrow NH_4^+ + OH^-$

In this case, the water molecule acts as the acid, donating a proton to the base NH3 to create the *ammonium ion* NH_4^+.

The foregoing examples illustrate several important aspects of the Brønsted-Lowry concept of acids and bases:

- A substance cannot act as an acid unless a proton acceptor (base) is present to receive the proton;
- A substance cannot act as a base unless a proton donor (acid) is present to supply the proton;
- Water plays a dual role in many acid-base reactions; H_2O can act as a proton acceptor (base) for an acid, or it can serve as a proton donor (acid) for a base (as we saw for ammonia.
- The *hydronium ion* H_3O^+ plays a central role in the acid-base chemistry of aqueous solutions.

Hydrogen ions cannot exist in water.

There is another serious problem with the Arrhenius view of an acid as a substance that dissociates in water to produce a hydrogen ion. The hydrogen ion is no more than a proton, a bare nucleus. Although it carries only a single unit of positive charge, this charge is concentrated into a volume of space that is only about a hundred-millionth as large as the volume occupied by the smallest atom. The resulting extraordinarily high charge density of the proton strongly attracts it to any part of a nearby atom or molecule in which there is an excess of negative charge. In the case of water, this will be the lone pair (unshared) electrons of the oxygen atom; the tiny proton will be buried within the lone pair and will form a shared-electron (coordinate) bond with it, creating a hydronium ion, H_3O^+. In a sense, H_2O is acting as a base here, and the product H_3O^+ is the conjugate acid of water.

Although other kinds of dissolved ions have water molecules bound to them more or less tightly, the interaction between H^+ and H_2O is so strong that writing "H+*(aq)*" hardly does it justice, although it is formally correct. The formula H_3O^+ more adequately conveys the sense that it is both a molecule in its own right, and is also the conjugate acid of water.

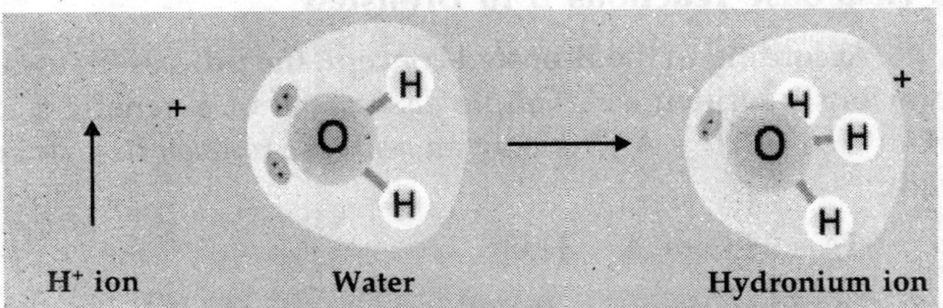

Fig. 9.1

The equation "HA → H^+ + A^-" is so much easier to write that chemists still use it to represent acid-base reactions in contexts in which the proton donor-acceptor mechanism does not need to be emphasized. Thus it is permissible to talk about "hydrogen ions" and use the formula H^+ in writing chemical equations as long as you remember that they are not to be taken literally in the context of aqueous solutions.

Interestingly, experiments indicate that the proton does not stick to a single H_2O molecule, but changes partners many times per second. This molecular promiscuity, a consequence of the uniquely small size and mass the proton, allows it to move through the solution by rapidly hopping from one H_2O molecule to the next, creating a new H_3O^+ ion as it goes. The overall effect is the same as if the H_3O^+ ion itself were moving. Similarly, a hydroxide ion, which can be considered to be a "proton hole" in the water, serves as a landing point for a proton from another H_2O molecule, so that the OH^- ion hops about in the same way.

Because hydronium- and hydroxide ions can "move without actually moving" and thus without having to plow their way through the solution by shoving aside water molecules as do other ions, solutions which are acidic or alkaline have extraordinarily high electrical conductivities.

3 Acid-base reactions *à la* Brønsted

According to the Brønsted concept, the process that was previously written as a simple *dissociation* of a generic acid HA ("HA → $H^+ + A^-$)" is now an *acid-base reaction* in its own right:

$$HA + H_2O \rightarrow A^- + H_3O^+$$

The idea, again, is that the proton, once it leaves the acid, must end up somewhere; it cannot simply float around as a free hydrogen ion.

Conjugate Pairs

A reaction of an acid with a base is thus a *proton exchange reaction*; if the acid is denoted by AH and the base by B, then we can write a generalized acid-base reaction as:

$$AH + B \rightarrow A^- + BH^+$$

Notice that the *reverse* of this reaction,

$$BH^+ + A^- \rightarrow B + AH^+$$

is also an acid-base reaction. Because all simple reactions can take place in both directions to some extent, it follows that transfer of a proton from an acid to a base must necessarily create a new pair of species that can, at least in principle, constitute an acid-base pair of their own.

10 Water pH

What is pH?

We learned in school that water, or H_2O, is composed of hydrogen and oxygen molecules. Neutral water is given a pH value of 7.0. It contains equal amounts of hydrogen ions (H^+) and hydroxide ions (OH^-). Dissolved chemicals and minerals change the balance of those ions from a perfectly neutral state.

Increase the amount of hydrogen ions (H^+), and the water becomes more acid ("low pH"). Increase the amount of hydroxide ions (OH^-), and the water becomes more alkaline ("high pH"). The further these values rise or fall, the more acid or alkaline the water becomes.

What is Normal pH?

There is no "normal" pH that applies to all fish. Because fish originate in ponds, rivers, streams, lakes, and oceans that have different pH levels, their needs are different. Saltwater fish prefer an alkaline pH of 8.0 or above. Freshwater fish thrive in a range lower than that, somewhere between 5.5 and 7.5, depending on the specific species.

Keep in mind that pH is not static, it changes over time, in fact it even changes over the course of a single day. Typically it drops at night and rises during the daytime. The pH will change as new fish are added or removed, as water is added or changed, and as the biological processes change in the tank.

Preferred pH of Common Frewhater Fish

— Angelfish 6.5-7.0

— Clown Loach 6.0-6.5

— Goldfish 7.0-7.5

— Harlequin 6.0-6.5

— Hachetfish 6.0-7.0

— Neon Tetra 5.8-6.2

— Plecostomus 5.0-7.0

— Silver Dollar 6.0-7.0

— Tiger Barb 6.0-6.5

— Zebra Danio 6.5-7.0

How Important is pH?

Changes in the pH, especially sudden changes, can prove harmful or even fatal to fish . As the pH rises it increases the toxicity of chemicals such as ammonia. It is an important factor to monitor during the break-in of a new tank. pH changes are particularly hard on young and sick fish. In a number of species of fish, breeding occurs only within a specific pH range.

If you are planning a new aquarium it's wise to know the pH of your water source, so you know before hand if it is compatible. Some fish such as Discus, and certain cichlids, thrive in a very narrow ranges of pH which should be taken into consideration when setting up their aquarium.

When moving fish from one aquarium to another it is important to match the pH levels. Sudden changes in pH account for many fish losses that occur when fish are brought home from a pet shop. Neon tetras are particularly sensitive to sudden changes in pH, and can easily be shocked when moved.

How often should we check pH?

pH should be tested at least once a month, preferably every two weeks to allow for detection of trends before they become a problem. Test results should be kept in a log book for future reference. Remember that because pH can vary based on time of day, testing at different times of day can yield different results even though nothing is wrong. For this reason testing should take place the same time of day, preferably in the afternoon.

Any time there is a fish illness or death, the pH should be tested. If the tank is treated with medication, the pH should be checked when treatment is begun, on the final day of treatment, and again a week later.

It is also wise to test your water just before purchasing new fish. Check with the shop where you are purchasing the fish. It's important that the pH of water the fish is currently in is not significantly different than the pH of your water at home.

Should pH be Altered?

I recommend sticking to the axiom of "if it's not broken, don't fix it". Don't spring to action simply because the textbook says the optimum pH for your fish is 6.4. and your water tests out at 6.0. As long as the pH is stable, and the fish show no signs of distress, it's best to leave the pH at it's natural level.

If the fish are not thriving, or if testing shows that a trend is occurring, such as a steady drop or rise in pH, the problem should be addressed. Proactive water care is always your best bet. Performing frequent partial water changes, and vacuuming the gravel are the most important things you can do to keep water pH stable.

pH is a measure of the acidity or basicity of a solution. It is defined as the cologarithm of the activity of dissolved hydrogen ions (H^+). Hydrogen ion activity coefficients cannot be measured experimentally, so they are based on theoretical calculations. The pH scale is not an absolute scale; it is relative to a set of standard solutions whose pH is established by international agreement.

The concept of pH was first introduced by Danish chemist Søren Peder Lauritz Sørensen at the Carlsberg Laboratory in 1909. Sørensen suggested the notation "PH" for convenience, standing for "power of hydrogen",using the cologarithm of the concentration of hydrogen ions in solution, p[H] Although this definition has been superseded p[H] can be measured if an electrode is calibrated with solution of known hydrogen ion concentration.

Pure water is said to be neutral. The pH for pure water at 25 °C (77 °F) is close to 7.0. Solutions with a pH less than 7 are said to be acidic and solutions with a pH greater than 7 are said to be basic or alkaline. pH measurements are important for medicine, biology, chemistry, food science, environmental science, oceanography and many other applications.

DEFINITIONS

pH

pH is defined as minus the decimal logarithm of the hydrogen ion activity in an aqueous solution. By virtue of its logarithmic nature, pH is a dimensionless quantity.

$$pH = -\log_{10}\left(aH^+\right) = \log_{10}\left(\frac{1}{aH^+}\right)$$

where a_H is the (dimensionless) activity of hydrogen ions. The reason for this definition is that a_H is a property of a single ion which can only be measured experimentally by means of an ion-selective electrode which responds, according to the Nernst equation, to hydogen ion activity. pH is commonly measured by means of a combined glass electrode, which measures the potential difference, or electromotive force, E, between an electrode sensitive to the hydrogen ion activity and a reference electrode, such as a calomel electrode or a silver chloride electrode. The combined glass electrode ideally follows the Nernst equation:

$$E = E^0 + \frac{RT}{nF}\ln\left(a_H\right);$$

$$\text{pH} = \frac{E^0 - E}{2.303\,RT/F}$$

where E is a measured potential , E^0 is the standard electrode potential, that is, the electode potential for the standard state in which the activity is one. R is the gas constant T is the temperature in Kelvin, F is the Faraday constant and n is the number of electrons transferred, one in this instance. The electrode potential, E, is proportional to the logarithm of the hydrogen ion activity.

This definition, by itself, is wholly impractical because the hydrogen ion activity is the product of the concentration and an activity coefficient. The single-ion activity coefficient of the hydrogen ion is a quantity which cannot be measured experimentally. To get round this difficulty the electrode is calibrated in terms of solutions of known activity.

The operational definition of pH is officially defined by International Standard ISO 31-8 as follows: For a solution X, first measure the electromotive force E_X of the galvanic cell.

reference electrode | concentrated solution of KCl || solution X | H_2 | Pt

and then also measure the electromotive force E_S of a galvanic cell that differs from the above one only by the replacement of the solution X of unknown pH, pH(X), by a solution S of a known standard pH, pH(S). The pH of X is then:

$$pH(X) - pH(S) = \frac{E_s - E_X}{2.303\, RT/F}$$

The difference between the pH of solution X and the pH of the standard solution depends only on the difference between two measured potentials. Thus, pH is obtained from a potential measured with an electrode calibrated against one or more pH standards; a pH meter setting is adjusted such that the meter reading for a solution of a standard is equal to the value pH(S). Values pH(S) for a range of standard solutions S, along with further details, are given in the IUPAC recommendations. The standard solutions are often described as standard buffer solution. In practice it is better to use two or more standard buffers to allow for small deviations from Nernst-law ideality in real electrodes. Note that because the temperature occurs in the defining equations, the pH of a solution is temperature-dependent.

Measurement of extremely low pH values, such as some very acidic mine waters requires special procedures. Calibration of the electrode in such cases can be done with standard solutions of concentrated sulfuric acid whose pH values can be calculated with using Pitzer parameters to calculate activity coefficients.

pH is an example of an acidity function. Hydrogen ion concentrations can be measured in non-aqueous solvents, but this leads, in effect, to a different acidity function because the standard state for a non-aqueous solvent is different from the standard state for water. Superacids are a class of non-aqueous acids for which the Hammett acidity function, H_0, has been developed.

p[H]

This was the original definition of Sørensen, which was superseded in favour of pH. However, it is possible to measure the concentration of hydrogen ions directly, if the electrode is calibrated in terms of hydrogen ion concentrations. One way to do this, which has been used extensively, is to titrate a solution of known concentration of a strong acid with a solution of known concentration of strong alkali in the presence of a relatively high concentration of background electrolyte. Since the concentrations of acid and alkali are known it is easy to calculate the concentration of hydrogen ions so that the measured potential can be correlated with concentrations. The calibration is usually carried out using a Gran plot. The calibration yields a value for the standard electrode potential, E^0, and a slope factor, f, so that the Nernst equation

$$E = E^0 + f\frac{RT}{nf}\log_e\left[H^+\right]$$

in the form can be used to derive hydrogen ion concentrations from experimental measurements of E. The slope factor is usually slightly less than one. A slope factor of less than 0.95 indicates that the electrode is not functioning correctly. The presence of background electrolyte ensures that the hydrogen ion activity coefficient is effectively constant during the titration. As it is constant its value can be set to one by defining the standard state as being the solution containing the background electrolyte. Thus, the effect of using this procedure is to make activity equal to the numerical value of concentration.

The difference between p[H] and pH is quite small. It has been stated that pH = p[H] + 0.04. Unfortunately it is common practice to use the term "pH" for both types of measurement.

pOH

pOH is sometimes used as a measure of the concentration of hydroxide ions, OH^-, or alkalinity. pOH is not measured independently, but is derived from pH. The concentration of hydroxide ions in water is related to the concentration of hydrogen ions by

$$[OH^-] = K_w/[H^+]$$

where K_w is the self-ionisation constant of water. Taking cologarithms

$$pOH = pK_w - pH.$$

So, at room temperature pOH ≈ 14 – pH. However this relationship is not strictly valid in other circumstances, such as in measurements of soil alkalinity.

Applications

Pure water has a pH around 7; the exact values depends on the temperature. When an acid is dissolved in water the pH will be less than 7 and when a base, or alkali is dissolved in water the pH will be greater than 7. A solution of a strong acid, such as hydrochloric acid, at concentration 1 mol dm^{-3} has a pH of 0. A solution of a strong alkali, such as sodium hydroxide, at concentration 1 mol dm^{-3} has a pH of 14. Thus, measured pH values will mostly lie in the range 0 to 14. Since pH is a logarithmic scale a difference of one pH unit is equivalent to a ten-fold difference in hydrogen ion concentration.

Because the glass electrode (and other ion selective electrodes) reponds to activity, the electrode should be calibrated in a medium similar to the one being investigated. For instance, if one wishes to measure the pH of a seawater sample, the electrode should be calibrated in a solution resembling seawater in its chemical composition.

An approximate measure of pH may be obtained by using a pH indicator. A pH indicator is a substance that changes colour aroud a particular pH value. It is a weak acid or weak base and the colour change occurs around 1 pH unit either side of itsacid dissociation constant, or pK_a, value. For example, the naturally occuring indicator litmus is red in acidic solutions (pH<7) and blue in alkaline (pH>7) solutions. Universal indicator consists of a mixture of indicators such that there is a continuous colour change from about pH 2 to pH 10. Universal indicator paper is simple paper that has been impregnated with universal indicator.

A solution whose pH is 7 is said to be neutral, that is, it is neither acidic nor basic. Water is subject to a self-ionisation process.

$$H_2O \rightleftharpoons H^+ + OH^-$$

The dissociation constant, K_W, has a value of about 10^{-14}, so in neutral solution of a salt both the hydrogen ion concentration and hoxide ion concentration are about 10^{-7} mol dm^{-3}. The pH of purewater decreases with increasing temperatures. For example, thepH of pure water at 50 °C is 6·55. Note, however, that water tat has been exposed to air is mildly acidic. This is because water absorbs carbon dioxide from the air, and carbon dioxie is an acid. After absorption it is slowly converted into the weak acid, carbonic acid, which then dissociates to liberate hydrogen ions.

$$CO_2 + H_2O \rightleftharpoons H_2CO_3 \rightleftharpoons HCO_3^- + H^+$$

The pH of distilled water at room temperature is about 5.7.

pH in Nature

pH-dpendent plant pigments that can be used as pH indicators occur in many plants, including hibiscus, marigold, red cabbage (anthocyanin) and red wine.

Seawater

The pH of seawater is very important and there is evidence for ocean acidification. Distinct pH scales exist depending on the method used to calibrate the electrode.

- Using standard buffers: The ionic strength of standard buffer solutions is much lower, at about 0.1 M, than that of seawater, which is about 0.7 M. Consequently they are not recommended for use in measuring the pH of seawater.
- A set of buffers based on artificial seawater was developed. This pH scale is referred to as the total scale, denoted by pHT. The total scale was defined using a medium containing sulfate ions, which are subject to the proton absorbing equilibrium $H^+ + SO_4^{2-} \leftrightarrows HSO_4^-$.
- The free scale, denoted by pH_F, omits the effect of sulfate ions and focuses solely on $[H^+]_F$, in principle making it a simpler representation of hydrogen ion concentration. Analytically, only $[H^+]_T$ can be determined therefore, $[H^+]_F$ must be estimated using the $[SO_4^{2-}]$ and the dissociation constant constant of HSO_4^-. The utility of this scale is limited by the complexity of the calculations. pH values measured on the the free scale differ by up to 0.12 pH units from both the total and seawater scales.
- The seawater scale, denoted by pHSWS , takes account of the fact that hydrogen fluoride is a weak acid, $H^+ + F^- \rightleftharpoons HF$.

However, the concentration of sulfate ions is about 400 times larger than the concentration of fluoride, so the difference between the total and seawater scales is very small.

Living Systems

The pH of different cellular compartments, body fluids, and organ is usually tightly regulated in a process called acid-base homeostasis.

The pH of blood is usually slightly basic with a value of pH 7.4. This value is often referred to as physiological pH in biology and medicine.

Plaque can create a local acidic environment that can result in tooth decay by demineralization.

Enzymes and other proteins have an optimum pH range and can became inactivated or denatured outside this range.

WATER CONDUCTIVITY

Definition and Description

Conductivity of a substance is defined as *'the ability or power to conduct or transmit heat, electricity, or sound'*. Its units are Siemens per meter [S/m] in SI and microohms per centimeter [mmho/cm] in U.S. customary units. Its symbol is k or s.

Electrical Conductivity (EC)

An electrical current results from the motion of electrically charged particles in response to forces that act on them from an applied electric field. Within most solid materials a current arise from the flow of electrons, which is called electronic conduction. In all conductors, semiconductors, and many insulated materials only electronic conduction exists, and the electrical conductivity is strongly dependant on the number of electrons available to participate to the conduction process. Most metals are extremely good conductors of electricity, because of the large number of free electrons that can be excited in an empty and available energy state.

In water and ionic materials or fluids a net motion of charged ions can occur. This phenomenon produce an electric current and is called ionic conduction.

Electrical conductivity is defined as the ratio between the current density (J) and the electric field intensity (e) and it is the opposite of the resistivity (r, [W*m]):

$s = J/e = 1/r$

Silver has the highest conductivity of any metals: 63 x 10^6 S/m.

Water Conductivity

Pure water is not a good conductor of electricity. Ordinary distilled water in equilibrium with carbon dioxide of the air has a conductivity of about 10×10^{-6} $W^{-1*}m^{-1}$ (20 dS/m). Because the electrical current is transported by the ions in solution, the conductivity increases as the concentration of ions increases.

Thus conductivity increases as water dissolved ionic species.

Typical conductivity of waters:

- Ultra pure water 5.5 · 10-6 S/m
- Drinking water 0.005-0.05 S/m
- Sea water 5 S/m

Electrical Conductivity and TDS

TDS or Total Dissolved Solids is a measure of the total ions in solution. EC is actually a measure of the ionic activity of a solution in term of its capacity to transmit current. In dilute solution, TDS and EC are reasonably comparable. The TDS of a water sample based on the measured EC value can be calculated using the following equation:

TDS (mg/l) = 0.5 × EC (dS/m or mmho/com)

or

= 0.5 * 1000 × EC (mS/cm)

The above relationship can also be used to check the acceptability of water chemical analyses. It does not apply to wastewater.

As the solution become more concentrated (TDS > 1000 mg/l, EC > 2000 ms/cm), the proximity of the solution ions to each other depresses their activity and consequently their ability to transmit current, although the physical amount of dissolved solids is not affected. At high TDS values, the ratio TDS/EC increases and the relationship tends toward TDS = 0.9 × EC.

In these cases the above-mentioned relationship should not be used and each sample should be characterized separately.

For water for agricultural and irrigation purpose the values for EC and TDS are related to each other and can be converted with an accuracy of about 10% using the following equation:

TDS (mg/l) = 640 × EC (ds/m or mmho/cm).

With the reverse osmosis process, water is forced in a semi-impermeable membrane leaving the impurities behind. This process is capable of removing 95-99% of TDS, providing pure or ultra-pure water.

Use Lenntech calculators to calculate the TDS content from water analysis and to convert TDS in EC ou visa versa.

Conductivity and Water Quality

Conductivity is a measurement of the ability of an aqueous solution to carry an electrical current. An ion is an atom of an element that has gained or lost an electron which will create a negative or positive state. For example, sodium chloride (table salt) consists of sodium ions (Na^+) and chloride ions (Cl^-) held together in a crystal. In water it breaks apart into an aqueous solution of sodium and chloride ions. This solution will conduct an electrical current. An equation which shows this is:

Na (atom) + Cl (atom) Na + Cl – (ionic crystal)

Na + Cl – (in a water solution) = Na + (ion) + Cl – (ion)

There are several factors that determine the degree to which water will carry an electrical current. These include:

1. the concentration or number of ions;
2. mobility of the ion;
3. oxidation state (valence) and;
4. temperature of the water.

Resistance, which is an electrical measurement expressed in ohms, is the opposite of conductivity. Conductivity is then expressed in reciprocal ohms. A more convenient unit of measurement in the chemical analysis of water is micromhos. The specific conductance or conductivity measurement is related to ionic strength and does not tell us what specific ions are present.

Methodology

The specific conductance of a sample is measured by a self-contained conductivity electrode.

Environmental Impact

Conductivity is a measurement used to determine a number of applications related to water quality. These are as follows:

1. determining mineralization: this is commonly called total dissolved solids. Total dissolved solids information is used to determine the overall ionic effect in a water

source. Certain physiological effects on plants and animals are often affected by the number of available ions in the water;

2. noting variation or changes in natural water and wastewaters quickly;
3. estimating the sample size necessary for other chemical analyses; and
4. determining amounts of chemical reagents or treatment chemicals to be added to a water sample.

Elevated dissolved solids can cause "mineral tastes" in drinking water. Corrosion or encrustation of metallic surfaces by waters high in dissolved solids causes problems with industrial equipment and boilers as well as domestic plumbing, hot water heaters, toilet flushing mechanisms, faucets, and washing machines and dishwashers.

Indirect effects of excess dissolved solids are primarily the elimination of desirable food plants and habitat-forming plant species. Agricultural uses of water for livestock watering are limited by excessive dissolved solids and high dissolved solids can be a problem in water used for irrigation.

11 Ocean Water

An ocean [from Greek, 'Okeanos' (Oceanus)] is a major body of saline water, and a principal component of the hydrosphere. Approximately 71% of the Earth's surface (an area of some 361 million square kilometers) is covered by ocean, a continuous body of water that is customarily divided into several principal oceans and smaller seas. More than half of this area is over 3,000 meters (9,800 ft) deep. Average oceanic salinity is around 35 parts per thousand (ppt) (3.5%), and nearly all seawater has a salinity in the range of 30 to 38 ppt.

Overview

Though generally recognized as several 'separate' oceans, these waters comprise one global, interconnected body of salt water often referred to as the World Ocean or global ocean. This concept of a global ocean as a continuous body of water with relatively free interchange among its parts is of fundamental importance to oceanography The major oceanic divisions are defined in part by the continents, various archipelagos, and other criteria. These divisions are (in descending order of size):

- *Pacific Ocean,* which separates Asia and Australia from Americas.
- *Atlantic Ocean,* which separates Americas from Eurasia and Africa.
- *Indian Ocean,* which washes upon southern Asia and separates Africa and Australia.
- *Southern Ocean,* sometimes subsumed as the southern portions of the Pacific, Atlantic, and Indian Oceans.
- *Arctic Ocean,* sometimes considered a sea of the Atlantic.

The Pacific and Atlantic may be further subdivided by the equator into northern and southern portions. Smaller regions of the oceans are called seas, gulfs, bays and other names. There are also some smaller bodies of saltwater that are on land and not interconnected with the World Ocean, such as the Aral Sea and the Great Salt Lake – though they may be referred to as 'seas', they are actually salt lakes.

As ocean covers most of Earth's surface, it has a significant impact on the biosphere. The evaporation of ocean water (as a component of the water cycle) is the source of most rainfall, and ocean temperatures determine climate and wind patterns. Life within the ocean had already evolved 3 billion years prior to the occurrence of animal and plant life on land. The ocean is home to many species of life throughout all aquatic layers. In addition, the amount of life and distance from the shore (abiotic component) affect the major distribution of marine biomes.

Geologically, an ocean is an area of oceanic crust covered by water. Oceanic crust is the thin layer of solidified volcanic basalt that covers the Earth's mantle where there are no continents. From this perspective, there are three oceans today: the World Ocean and the Caspian and Black Seas, the latter two having been formed by the collision of Cimmeria with Laurasia. The Mediterranean Sea is very nearly a discrete ocean, being connected to the World Ocean through the Strait of Gibraltar, and indeed several times over the last few million years movement of the African continent has closed the strait off entirely. The Black Sea is connected to the Mediterranean through the Bosporus, but this is in effect a natural canal cut through continental rock some 7,000 years ago, rather than a piece of oceanic sea floor like the Strait of Gibraltar.

Physical Properties

The area of the World Ocean is 361 million square kilometers (139 million sq mi) its volume is approximately 1.3 billion cubic kilometers (310 million cu mi). This can be thought of as a cube of water with an edge length of 1,111 kilometers (690 mi). Its average depth is 3,790 meters (12,430 ft) Nearly half of the world's marine waters are over 3,000 meters (9,800 ft) deep. The vast expanses of deep ocean (anything below 200m) cover about 66% of the Earth's surface This does not include seas not connected to the World Ocean, such as the Caspian Sea.

The total mass of the hydrosphere is about 1.4×10^{21} kilograms, which is about 0.023% of the Earth's total mass. Less than three per cent is freshwater; the rest is saltwater, mostly in the ocean.

Colour

A common misconception is that the oceans are blue primarily because the sky is blue. In fact, water has a very slight blue color that can only be seen in large volumes. While the sky's reflection does contribute to the blue appearance of the surface, it is not the primary cause. The primary cause is the absorption by the water molecules' nuclei of red photons from the incoming light, the only known example of color in nature resulting from vibrational, rather than electronic, dynamics.

Glow

A number of sailors and professional mariners have reported that the ocean often emits a visible glow, or luminescence, which extends for miles at night. In 2005, scientists announced that for the first time,. photographic evidence had been obtained of this glow. It may be due to bioluminescence.

Exploration

Travel on the surface of the ocean through the use of boats dates back to prehistoric times, but only in modern times has extensive underwater travel become possible.

The deepest point in the ocean is the Marianas Trench located in the Pacific Ocean near the Northern Mariana Islands. It has a maximum depth of 10,923 meters (35,838 ft) It was fully surveyed in 1951 by the British naval vessel, "Challenger II" which gave its name to the deepest part of the trench, the "Challenger Deep". In 1960, the Trieste successfully reached the bottom of the trench, manned by a crew of two men.

Much of the bottom of the world's oceans are unexplored and unmapped. A global image of many underwater features larger than 10 kilometers (6 mi) was created in 1995 based on gravitational distortions of the nearby sea surface.

Regions

Oceans are divided into numerous regions depending on the physical and biological conditions of these areas. The pelagic zone includes all open ocean regions, and can be subdivided into further regions categorized by depth and light abundance. The photic zone covers the oceans from surface level to 200 metres down. This is the region where the photosynthesis most commonly occurs and therefore contains the largest biodiversity in the ocean. Since plants can only survive with photosynthesis any life found lower than this must either rely on material floating down from above or find another primary source; this often comes in the form of hydrothermal vents in what is known as the aphotic zone (all depths exceeding 200m). The pelagic part of the photic zone is known as the epipelagic. The pelagic part of the aphotic zone can be further divided into regions that succeed each other vertically. The mesopelagic is the uppermost region, with its lowermost boundary at a thermocline of 12 °C, which, in the tropics generally lies between 700 and 1,000 m. After that is the bathypelagic lying between 10 °C and 4 °C, or between 700 or 1,000 m and 2,000 or 4,000 m. Lying along the top of the abyssal plain is the abyssalpelagic, whose lower boundary lies at about 6,000 m. The final zone falls into the oceanic trenches, and is known as the hadalpelagic. This lies between 6,000 m and 10,000 m and is the deepest oceanic zone.

Along with pelagic aphotics zones there are also benthic aphotic zones, these correspond to the three deepest zones. The bathyal zone covers the continental slope and the rise down to about 4,000 m. The abyssal zone covers the abyssal plains between 4,000 and 6,000 m. Lastly, the hadal zone corresponds to the hadalpelagic zone which is found in the oceanic trenches. The pelagic zone can also be split into two subregions, the neritic zone and the oceanic zone. The neritic encompasses the water mass directly above the continental shelves, while the oceanic zone includes all the completely open water. In contrast, the littoral zone covers the region between low and high tide and represents the transitional area between marine and terrestrial conditions. It is also known as the intertidal zone because it is the area where tide level affects the conditions of the region.

Climate Effects

One of the most dramatic forms of weather occurs over the oceans: tropical cyclones (also called "typhoons" and "hurricanes" depending upon where the system forms). Ocean currents greatly affect the Earth's climate by transferring warm or cold air and precipitation to coastal regions, where they may be carried inland by winds. The Antarctic Circumpolar Current encircles that continent, influencing the area's climate and connecting currents in several oceans.

Biology

Lifeforms native to oceans include (among others):

- Radiata
- Fish
- Cetacea such as whales, dolphins and porpoises
- Cephalopods such as the octopus
- Crustaceans such as lobsters, shrimp and krill
- Marine worms
- Plankton
- Echinoderms (brittle star, starfish, sea cucumber, sand dollar)

Economy

The oceans are essential to transportation: most of the world's goods are moved by ship between the world's seaports. Important ship canals include the Saint Lawrence Seaway, Panama Canal, and Suez Canal. They are also an important source of valuable food items for the fishing industry. Some of these are shrimp, fish, crabs and lobster.

Ancient Oceans

Continental drift has reconfigured the Earth's oceans, joining and splitting ancient oceans to form the current oceans. Ancient oceans include:

- *Bridge River Ocean,* the ocean between the ancient Insular Islands and North America.
- *Iapetus Ocean,* the southern hemisphere ocean between Baltica and Avalonia.
- *Panthalassa,* the vast world ocean that surrounded the Pangaea supercontinent.
- *Rheic Ocean*
- *Slide Mountain Ocean,* the ocean between the ancient Intermontane Islands and North America.
- *Tethys Ocean,* the ocean between the ancient continents of Gondwana and Laurasia.
- *Khanty Ocean,* the ocean between Baltica and Siberia.
- *Mirovia,* the ocean that surrounded the Rodinia supercontinent.
- *Paleo-Tethys Ocean,* the ocean between Gondwana and the Hunic terranes.
- *Proto-Tethys Ocean.*
- Pan-African Ocean, the ocean that surrounded the Pannotia supercontinent.
- *Superocean,* the ocean that surrounds a global supercontinent.
- *Ural Ocean,* the ocean between Siberia and Baltica.

Extraterrestrial Oceans

Earth is the only known planet with liquid water on its surface and is certainly the only one in our own solar system. However, liquid water is thought to be present under the surface of the Galilean moons Europa and, with less certainty, Callisto and Ganymede. Geysers have been found on Enceladus, though these may not involve bodies of liquid water. Other icy moons may have once had internal oceans that have now frozen, such as Triton. The planets

Uranus and Neptune may also possess large oceans of liquid water under their thick atmospheres, though their internal structure is not well understood at this time.

There is currently much debate over whether Mars once had an ocean of water in its northern hemisphere, and over what happened to it if it did; recent findings by the Mars Exploration Rover mission indicate it had some long-term standing water in at least one location, but its extent is not known.

Astronomers believe that Venus had liquid water and perhaps oceans in its very early history. If they existed, all trace of them seems to have vanished in later resurfacing.

Liquid hydrocarbons are thought to be present on the surface of Titan, though it may be more accurate to describe them as "lakes" rather than an "ocean." The Cassini-Huygens space mission initially discovered only what appeared to be dry lakebeds and empty river channels, suggesting that Titan had lost what surface liquids it might have had. A more recent fly-by of Titan made by Cassini has produced radar images that strongly suggest hydrocarbon lakes near the polar regions where it is colder. Titan is also thought likely to have a subterranean water ocean under the mix of ice and hydrocarbons that forms its outer crust.

Beyond the solar system, Gliese 581 c is at the right distance from its sun for liquid water to exist on the planet's surface. Since it does not transit its sun, there is no way to know if there is any water there. However, the greenhouse effect of Gliese 581 c would make it too hot for oceans to exist on the surface. However, the greenhouse effect of Gliese 581 d may bring temperatures suitable enough for the existence of surface oceans. HD 209458 b may have water vapour in its atmosphere—this is currently being disputed. Gliese 436 b is believed to have "hot ice." Neither of these planets are cool enough for liquid water—but if water molecules exist there, they are also likely to be found on planets at a suitable temperature.

SALINITY

Salinity is the saltiness or dissolved salt content of a body of water. Salinity in Australian English and North American English may also refer to the salt in soil.

Definitions

The technical term for saltiness in the ocean is halinity, from the fact that halides - chloride specifically - are the most abundant anions in the mix of dissolved elements. In oceanography, it has been traditional to express salinity not as percent, but as parts per thousand (ppt or ‰), which is approximately grams of salt per liter of solution. Other disciplines use chemical analyses of solutions, and thus salinity is frequently reported in mg/L or ppm (parts per million). Prior to 1978, salinity or halinity was expressed as ‰ usually based on the electrical conductivity ratio of the sample to "Copenhagen water", an artificial sea water manufactured to serve as a world "standard". In 1978, oceanographers redefined salinity in the Practical Salinity Scale (PSS) as the conductivity ratio of a sea water sample to a standard KCl solution . Ratios have no units, so it is not the case that a salinity of 35 exactly equals 35 grams of salt per litre of solution.

These seemingly esoteric approaches to measuring and reporting salt concentrations may appear to obscure their practical use; but it must be remembered that salinity is the sum weight of many different elements within a given volume of water. It has always been the case that to get a precise salinity as a concentration and convert this to an amount of substance (sodium chloride, for instance) required knowing much more about the sample and the measurement than just the weight of the solids upon evaporation (one method of determining "salinity"). For example, volume is influenced by water temperature; and the composition of the salts is not a constant (although generally very much the same throughout the world ocean). Saline waters from inland seas can have a composition that differs from that of the ocean. For the latter reason, these waters are termed saline as differentiated from ocean waters, where the term haline applies (although is not universally used).

Contour lines of constant salinity are called isohales.

Systems of Classification of Water Bodies based upon Salinity

Marine waters are those of the ocean, another term for which is euhaline seas. The salinity of euhaline seas is 30 to 35. Brackish seas or waters have salinity in the range of 0.5 to 29 and metahaline seas from 36 to 40. These waters are all regarded as thalassic because their salinity is derived from the ocean and defined as homoiohaline if salinity does not vary much over time (essentially invariant). The table on the right, modified from Por (1972), follows the "Venice system" (1959).

In contrast to homoiohaline environments are certain poikilohaline environments (which may also be thallassic) in which the salinity variation is biologically significance Poikilohaline water salinities may range anywhere from 0.5 to greater than 300. The important characteristic is that these waters tend to vary in salinity over some biologically meaningful range seasonally or on some other roughly comparable time scale. Put simply, these are bodies of water with quite variable salinity.

Highly saline water, from which salts crystallize (or are about to), is referred to as brine.

Environmental Considerations

Salinity is an ecological factor of considerable importance, influencing the types of organisms that live in a body of water. As well, salinity influences the kinds of plants that will grow either in a water body, or on land fed by a water (or by a groundwater). A plant adapted to saline conditions is called a halophyte. Organisms (mostly bacteria) that can live in very salty conditions are classified as extremophiles, halophiles specifically. An organism that can withstand a wide range of salinities is euryhaline.

Salt is difficult to remove from water, and salt content is an important factor in water use (such as potability).

FRESHWATER

Freshwater is a word that refers to bodies of water such as ponds, lakes, rivers and streams containing low concentrations of dissolved salts and other total dissolved solids. In other words, the term excludes seawater and brackish water. Freshwater can also be the output of desalinated seawater.

Freshwater is an important renewable resource, necessary for the survival of most terrestrial organisms, and is required by humans for drinking and agriculture, among many uses. The UN estimates that about 18 percent of the world's population lacks access to safe drinking water.

Numerical Definition

Frshwater is defined as water with less than 0.5 parts per thousand dissolved salts Freshwater bodies include lakes and ponds, rivers, some bodies of underground water and many kinds of man-made freshwater bodies, such as canals, ditches an reservoirs. The ultimate source of freshwater is the precipitation of atmosphere in the form of rain and snow.

Water Distribution

Access to fresh water is a critical issue for the survival of many species including humans, who must drink it in order to survive. Only three per cent of the water on Earth is freshwater in nature, and about two-thirds of this is frozen in glaciers and polar ice caps. Most of the rest is underground and only 0.3 per cent is surface water. Freshwater lakes, most notably Lake Baikal in Russa and the Great Lakes in North America, contain seven-eights of this fresh surface water. Swamps have most of the balance with only a small amount in rivers, most notably the Amazn River. The atmosphere contains 0.04% water. In areas with no freshwater on the ground surface, freshwater derived from precipitation may, because of its lower density, overlie saline ground water in lenses or layers.

Aquatic Organisms

Freshwater creates a hypotonic environment for aquatic organisms. This is problematic for some organisms, whose cell membranes will burst if excess water is not excreted. Some protists accomplish this using contractile vacuoles, while freshwater fish excrete excess water via the kidney. Although most aquatic organisms have a limited ability to regulate their osmotic balance and therefore can only live within a narrow range of salinity, diadromous fish have the ability to migrate between freshwater and saline water bodies. During these migrations they undergo changes to adapt to the surroundings of the changed salinities; these processes are hormonally controlled. The eel (*Anguilla anguilla*) uses the hormone prolactin, while in salmon (*Salmo salar*) the hormone cortisol plays a key role during this process.

Natural Activity Against Human Activity

Freshwater is a highly valuable natural resource that has a variety of use in both human and nature activity. Freshwater is an important natural resource that allow local ecosystem of plantations of species to survive. Flows of freshwater also bring soils and nutrients that are necessary in the growth and increase of local plantation which forms food chain that ensure the food supply of local species. However, the overuse of water in human activity such as irrigation, production of products in industries and drinking water had cause a huge damage in freshwater and nature ecosystem. Changes in the contamination of freshwater results in massive diebacks of living organism, because of either too much or too little freshwater was contained in water source The overuse of freshwater lowered the quantities of freshwater available in the freshwater ecosystem which caused the crush of balance between human society and nature. As a result, large amount of species and plantations became endangered and even extinct from the world and the local environment due to the large scale of change. Usage of freshwater must be controlled before it causes damage in environment and human society.

Pollution from human activity, including oil spills, also presents a problem for freshwater resources. The largest oil spill that has ever occurred in freshwater was caused by a Shell tank ship in Magdalena, Argentina, on January 15, 1999, polluting the environment, drinkable water, plants and animals.

Agriculture-change of Landscape

Changing landscape for the use of agriculture creates a great effect on flow of freshwater and surrounding. Reshaping a large scale of landscape in creating lands that are suitable for agriculture changed the flow and sustainability of freshwater which result in effecting the sustainability of the local ecosystem. Changes in landscape through the remove of trees and soils changed the local environments flow of freshwater and also effect the cycle of freshwater. As a result more freshwater are consumed and stored in soil which benefits agriculture. However, since agriculture was the human activity that consumes the most freshwater would be used up completely which result in scarcity and destroy of local ecosystem. Similar to events happening in Australia where too much land and freshwater flow are restructured for the use of agriculture, which ends up causing 33% of lands area at risk of salinization and scarcity Redesigning lands for the maximum use of agriculture will certainly bring a great damage to the environment and reduces the available freshwater supply since freshwater is a limiting natural resource.

Limiting Resource

Freshwater is a renewable but limiting natural resource. As availability of freshwater in freshwater ecosystems decreases, nature restores it through the water cycle in the form of precipitation. Freshwater can only be renewed through the process of the water cycle, where water from seas, lakes, rivers, and dams evaporates, forms clouds, and returns to water sources as precipitation. However, if more freshwater is consumed through human activities than is restored by nature, the result is that the quantity of freshwater available in lakes, rivers, dams and underground waters is reduced which can cause serious damage to the surrounding environment.

Freshwater Management Programme

Development of freshwater managing program helps to maintain and restore world's freshwater and freshwater ecosystem. As the world population increases more and more freshwater are needed to satisfied world demand of freshwater which reduce the quantity of available freshwater and also caused a great damage in nature environment. In order to restore the freshwater and freshwater ecosystem six steps are taken to develop the freshwater management program. In the first step of developing freshwater management program the flow of freshwater and the maximum amount of freshwater needed for the environment was estimated. This ensure the nature environment, local plantation and species received enough freshwater that are needed for survival. In the second step of the process influence of human activity and the amount of freshwater human needs was estimated to ensure the supply of freshwater for both drinking and human activities. In the third step the location of the place that the program is going to take place is identify and compared to the previous estimate. By this way incorrect estimate can be corrected to ensure the environment receive the maximum amount of freshwater that it needs. In the forth step a detail outline of the plan that matches the collected data, estimation, and government's requirement were developed. In the fifth step the program are tested in a simple freshwater experiment and results are observed to improve and also correct any mistake that occur in the plan. In the last step the planed was retested and more research was made to improve and make sure the plane function would function correctly. After that the environment's adoptability to the program are examined to ensure the plan contribute no further damage to the environment. Freshwater management program would certainly contribute a great effort in restoring and maintaining the world's available freshwater and freshwater ecology.

Freshwater management program must be created through worldwide vision. In order to create a successful water management program, the program manager must never create the program through an economic view. Creating a water management program through economic point of view brought only a short term success in restoring freshwater and freshwater ecosystem. However, by having a worldwide view and consider the flow of freshwater as bloodstream of the biosphere's capacity and breath of the Earth, an efficient and effective water management program can be created. Have a worldwide view and consider flows of freshwater as breath of the atmosphere and bloodstream of earth allows the program manager to find out what the environment really need in restoring its freshwater and ecosystem. The worldwide view also allowed the program manager to understand the difference between each freshwater ecosystem and helps to develop plans that will work efficiently in the environment. Worldwide view is the key to develop a successful water management program.

Creating an effective water management program benefit both presents and future's human society and nature environment. As the global population increase the limiting water resource will become even more limiting. The greenhouse gases produced by human will also contribute a great effect to global warming which will cause the ice and glacier in North Pole and South Pole to melt. The melt of ice will result in increase of global sea level which might cover the land and mixed with freshwater. Developing an effective water management program helps not just in restoring the freshwater and freshwater ecosystem but also helps in reducing greenhouse gasses through the increase of plantation. Water management program will certainly contribute a lot in restoring and maintaining global freshwater supply and nature.

12 Vitamins, Water-Soluble

Vitamins are essential organic substances that are needed in small amounts in the diet for the normal function, growth, and maintenance of body tissues. Water-soluble vitamins consist of the B vitamins and vitamin C. With exception of vitamin B_6 and B_{12}, they are readily excreted in urine without appreciable storage, so frequent consumption becomes necessary. They are generally nontoxic when present in excess of needs, although symptoms may be reported in people taking megadoses of niacin, vitamin C, or pyridoxine (vitamin B_6). All the B vitamins function as coenzymes or cofactors, assisting in the activity of important enzymes and allowing energy-producing reactions to proceed normally. As a result, any lack of water-soluble vitamins mostly affects growing or rapidly metabolizing tissues such as skin, blood, the digestive tract, and the nervous system. Water-soluble vitamins are easily lost with overcooking.

Thiamin (Vitamin B_1)

Thiamin functions as the coenzyme thiamin pyrophosphate (TPP) in the metabolism of carbohydrate and in conduction of nerve impulses. Thiamin deficiency causes beri-beri, which is frequently seen in parts of the world where polished (white) rice or unenriched white flour are predominantly eaten. There are three basic expressions of beriberi: childhood, wet, and dry. Childhood beriberi stunts growth in infants and children. Wet beriberi is the classic form, with swelling due to fluid retention (edema) in the lower limbs that spreads to the upper body, affecting the heart and leading to heart failure. Dry beriberi affects peripheral nerves, initially causing tingling or burning sensations in the lower limbs and progressing to nerve degeneration, muscle wasting, and weight loss. Thiamine-deficiency disease in North America commonly occurs in people with heavy alcohol consumption and is called Wernicke-Korsakoff syndrome. It is caused by poor food intake and by decreased absorption and increased excretion caused by alcohol consumption.

Riboflavin (Vitamin B_2)

Riboflavin is stable when heated in ordinary cooking, unless the food is exposed to ultraviolet radiation (sunlight). To prevent riboflavin breakdown, riboflavin-rich foods such as milk, milk products, and cereals are packaged in opaque containers. Riboflavin is a component of two coenzymes—flavin mononucleotide (FMN) and flavin adenine dinucleotide (FAD)—that act as hydrogen carriers when carbohydrates and fats are used to produce energy. It is helpful in maintaining good vision and healthy hair, skin and nails, and it is necessary for normal cell growth.

Riboflavin deficiency causes a condition known as ariboflavinosis, which is marked by cheilosis (cracks at the corners of the mouth), oily scaling of the skin, and a red, sore tongue. In addition, cataracts may occur more frequently with riboflavin deficiency. A deficiency of this nutrient is usually a part of multinutrient deficiency and does not occur in isolation. In North America, it is mostly observed in alcoholics, elderly persons with low income or depression, and people with poor eating habits, particularly those who consume highly refined and fast foods and those who do not consume milk and milk products.

Niacin (Vitamin B_3)

Niacin exists in two forms, nicotinic acid and nicotinamide. Both forms are readily absorbed from the stomach and the small intestine. Niacin is stored in small amounts in the liver and transported to tissues, where it is converted to coenzyme forms. Any excess is excreted in urine. Niacin is one of the most stable of the B vitamins. It is resistant to heat and light, and to both acid and alkali environments. The human body is capable of converting the amino acid tryptophan to niacin when needed. However, when both tryptophan and niacin are deficient, tryptophan is used for protein synthesis.

There are two coenzyme forms of niacin: nicotinamide adenine dinucleotide (NAD+) and nicotinamide adenine dinucleotide phophate (NADP+). They both help break down and utilize proteins, fats, and carbohydrates for energy. Niacin is essential for growth and is involved in hormone synthesis.

Pellagra results from a combined deficiency of niacin and tryptophan. Long-term deficiency leads to central nervous system dysfunction manifested as confusion, apathy, disorientation, and eventually coma and death.

Pellagra is rarely seen in industrialized countries, where it may be observed in people with rare disorder of tryptophan metabolism (Hartnup's disease), alcoholics, and those with diseases that affect food intake.

Recommended intake is expressed as milligrams of niacin equivalents (NE) to account for niacin synthesized from tryptophan. High doses taken orally as nicotinic acid at 1.5 to 2 grams per day can decrease cholesterol and triglyceride levels, and along with diet and exercise can slow or reverse the progression of heart disease.

Table 12.1: Water soluble vitamines

Vitamin	Deficiency	Recommended daily intake	Food sources	Toxicity
Thiamine (Vitamin B_1)	Beri-beri: anorexia, weight loss, weakness, peripheral neuropathy Wernicke-Korsakoff syndrome: staggered gait, cross eyes, dementia, disorientation, memory loss	Infants: 0.2-0.3 mg Children: 0.5-0.6 mg Adolescents: 0.9-1.2 mg Men: 1.2 mg Women: 1.1 mg Pregnant/Lactating Women: 1.4 mg	Pork/pork products, beef, liver, yeast/baked products, enriched and whole gain cereals, nuts and seeds	None reported
Riboflavin (Vitamin B_2)	Ariboflavinosis: inflammation of tongue (glossitis), cracks at corners of mouth (cheilosis) dermatitis, growth retardation, conjunctivitis, nerve damage	Infants: 0.3-0.4 mg Children: 0.5-0.6 mg Adolescents: 0.9-1.3 mg Men: 1.3 mg Women: 1.1 mg Pregnant Women: 1.4 mg Lactating Women: 1.6 mg	Milk, egg, mushrooms, whole grains, enriched grains, green leafy vegetables, yeast, liver and oily fish	None reported

(Contd...)

Vitamin	Deficiency	Recommended daily intake	Food sources	Toxicity
Niacin (Vitamin B_3)	Pellagra: diarrhoea dematitis, dementia, and death	Infants: 2-4 mg NE Children: 6-8 mg NE Adolescents: 12-16 mg NE Men: 16 mg NE Women: 14 mg NE Pregnant Women: 18 mg NE Lactating Women: 17 mg NE	Meat, poultry fish, yeast, enriched and whole grain breads and cereals, peanuts, mushrooms, milk and egg (tryptophan)	Flushing of skin, itching, nausea & vomiting, and liver damage occurs at intake over 35 mg/day from supplements
Pantothenic acid (Vitamin B_5)	Rare Children: 2-3 mg Adolescents: 4-5 mg Men & Women: 5 mg Pregnant Women: 6 mg Lactating Women: 7 mg	Infants: 1.7-1.8 mg in foods	Widely distributed	None reported
Biotin (Vitamin B_8)	Infants: Dermatitis, convulsions, hair loss (alopecia), neurological disorders, impaired growth	Infants: 5-6 μg children: 8-12 μg Adolescents: 20-25 μg Men & Women: 30 μg Pregnant Women: 30 μg Lactating Women: 35 μg	Whole grains, eggs, nuts and seeds, widely distributed in small amounts	Net known

(Contd...)

Vitamin	Deficiency	Recommended daily intake	Food sources	Toxicity
Vitamin B_6	Dermatitis, anemia, convulsion depression, confusion, decline in immune function	Infants: 0.1-0.3 mg Children: 0.5-0.6 mg Adolescents: 1.0-1.3 mg Men & Women (19-50 years): 1.3 mg Men over 50 years: 1.4 mg Women over 50 years: 1.3 mg Pregnant Women: 1.9 mg Lactating Women: 1.2 mg	Meat, fish poultry, spinach, potatoes, bananas, avocados, sunflower seeds	None from foods, excess intake above 100 mg/day from supplements causes neuropathy (nerve destruction) and skin lesions
Folate	Megaoblastic (macrocytic) anemia, abdominal pain, diarrhoea birth defects	Infants: 65-80 µg Children: 150-200 µg Adolescents: 300-400 µg Men & Women: 400 µg/day Pregnant Women: 600 µg Lactating Women: 500 µg	Ready-to-eat breakfast cereals, enriched grain products, green vegetables, liver, legumes, oranges. The use of fortified foods and encouraged for all women of child bearing age (15-45 years)	None (up to 5 mg/day); intake from fortified food and supplements over 1000 µg/day, not including food; folate masks vitamin B_{12} deficiency allowing progression of neurological damage Supplements containing >400 µg available by prescription only

Vitamin	Deficiency	Recommended daily intake	Food sources	Toxicity
Vitamin B_{12}	Pernicious Anemia: macrocytic anemia nervous system disturbances; paresthesia (tingling and numbness in limbs), difficulty walking, loss of bowel and bladder control dementia	Infants: 0.4-0.5 µg Children: 0.9 – 1.2 µg Adolescents: 1.8 µg Men & Women: 2.4 µg Pregnant Women: 2.6 µg Lactating Women: 2.8 µg	Meat, fish, poultry, ready-to-eat fortified breakfast cereals, eggs fermented dairy products (cheese, yogurt, etc). The use of fortified foods and supplements are recommended for adults 51 and over	None reported
Vitamin C	Scurvy: fatigue, poor wound healing, pinpoint hemorrhages around hair follicles on back of arms & legs, bleeding gums & joints	Infants: 40-50 mg Children: 15-25 mg Adolescents: 45-75 mg Men: 90 mg Women: 75 mg Pregnant Women: 80-85 mg Lactating Women: 115-120 mg Smokers: +35 mg	Citrus fruits, strawberries, broccoli, green	Megadoses over 2 g/day causes nausea, abdominal cramps and diarrhea.

The nicotinamide form of niacin in multivitamin and B-complex tablets do not work for this purpose. Supplementation should be under a physician's guidance.

Pantothenic Acid (Vitamin B_5)

Pantothenic acid is stable in moist heat. It is destroyed by vinegar (acid), baking soda (alkali), and dry heat. Significant losses occur during the processing and refining of foods. Pantothenic acid is released from coenzyme A in food in the small intestine. After absorption, it is transported to tissues, where coenzyme A is resynthesized. Coenzyme A is essential for the formation of energy as adenosine triphosphate (ATP) from carbohydrate, protein, alcohol, and fat. Coenzyme A is also important in the synthesis of fatty acids, cholesterol, steroids, and the neurotransmitter acetylcholine, which is essential for transmission of nerve impulses to muscles. Dietary deficiency occurs in conjunction with other B-vitamin deficiencies. In studies, experimentally induced deficiency in humans has resulted in headache, fatigue, impaired muscle coordination, abdominal cramps, and vomiting.

Biotin (Vitamin B_8)

Biotin is the most stable of B vitamins. It is commonly found in two forms: the free vitamin and the protein-bound coenzyme form called biocytin. Biotin is absorbed in the small intestine, and it requires digestion by enzyme biotinidase, which is present in the small intestine. Biotin is synthesized by bacteria in the large intestine, but its absorption is questionable. Biotincontaining coenzymes participate in key reactions that produce energy from carbohydrate and synthesize fatty acids and protein. Avidin is a protein in raw egg white, which can bind to the biotin in the stomach and decrease its absorption. Therefore, consumption of raw whites is of concern due to the risk of becoming biotin deficient. Cooking the egg white, however, destroys avidin. Deficiency may develop in infants born with a genetic defect that results in reduced levels of biotinidase. In the past, biotin deficiency was observed in infants fed biotin-deficient formula, so it is now added to infant formulas and other baby foods.

Vitamin B_6

Vitamin B_6 is present in three forms: pyridoxal, pyridoxine, and pyridoxamine. All forms can be converted to the active vitamin-B_6 coenzyme in the body. Pyridoxal phosphate (PLP) is the predominant biologically active form. Vitamin B6 is not stable in heat or in alkaline conditions, so cooking and food processing reduce its content in food. Both coenzyme and free forms are absorbed in the small intestine and transported to the liver, where they are phosphorylated and released into circulation, bound to albumin for transport to tissues. Vitamin B6 is stored in the muscle and only excreted in urine when intake is excessive.

PLP participates in amino acid synthesis and the interconversion of some amino acids. It catalyzes a step in the synthesis of hemoglobin, which is needed to transport oxygen in blood. PLP helps maintain blood glucose levels by facilitating the release of glucose from liver and muscle glycogen. It also plays a role in the synthesis of many neurotransmitters important for brain function. This has led some physicians to prescribe megadoses of B_6 to patients with psychological problems such as depression and mood swings, and to some women for premenstrual syndrome (PMS). It is unclear, however, whether this therapy is effective. PLP participates in the conversion of the amino acid tryptophan to niacin and helps avoid niacin deficiency. Pyridoxine affects immune function, as it is essential for the formation of a type of white blood cell.

Populations at risk of vitamin-B_6 deficiency include alcoholics and elderly persons who consume an inadequate diet. Individuals taking medication to treat Parkinson's disease or tuberculosis may take extra vitamin B6 with physician supervision. Carpal tunnel syndrome, a nerve disorder of the wrist, has also been treated with large daily doses of B_6. However, data on its effectiveness are conflicting.

Folic Acid, Folate, Folacin (Vitamin B_9)

Folacin or folate, as it is usually called, is the form of vitamin B_9 naturally present in foods, whereas folic acid is the synthetic form added to fortified foods and supplements. Both forms are absorbed in the small intestine and stored in the liver. The folic acid form, however, is more efficiently absorbed and available to the body. When consumed in excess of needs, both forms are excreted in urine and easily destroyed by heat, oxidation, and light.

All forms of this vitamin are readily converted to the coenzyme form called tetrahydrofolate (THFA), which plays a key role in transferring single-carbon methyl units during the synthesis of DNA and RNA, and in interconversions of amino acids. Folate also plays an important role in the synthesis of neurotransmitters. Meeting folate needs can improve mood and mental functions.

Folate deficiency is one of the most common vitamin deficiencies. Early symptoms are nonspecific and include tiredness, irritability, and loss of appetite. Severe folate deficiency leads to macrocytic anemia, a condition in which cells in the bone marrow cannot divide normally and red blood cells remain in a large immature form called *macrocytes*. Large immature cells also appear along the length of the gastrointestinal tract, resulting in abdominal pain and diarrhea.

Pregnancy is a time of rapid cell multiplication and DNA synthesis, which increases the need for folate. Folate deficiency may lead to neural tube defects such as spina bifida (failure of the spine to close properly during the first month of pregnancy) and anencephaly (closure of the neural tube during fetal development, resulting in part of the cranium not being formed). Seventy percent of these defects could be avoided by adequate folate status before conception, and it is recommended that all women of childbearing age consume at least 400 micrograms (μg) of folic acid each day from fortified foods and supplements. Other groups at risk of deficiency include elderly persons and persons suffering from alcohol abuse or taking certain prescription drugs.

Vitamin B_{12}.

Vitamin B_{12} is found in its free-vitamin form, called cyanocobalamin, and in two active coenzyme forms. Absorption of vitamin B_{12} requires the presence of *intrinsic factor,* a protein synthesized by acid-producing cells of the stomach. The vitamin is absorbed in the terminal portion of the small intestine called the ileum. Most of body's supply of vitamin B_{12} is stored in the liver.

Vitamin B_{12} is efficiently conserved in the body, since most of it is secreted into bile and reabsorbed. This explains the slow development (about two years) of deficiency in people with reduced intake or absorption. Vitamin B_{12} is stable when heated and slowly loses its activity when exposed to light, oxygen, and acid or alkaline environments.

Vitamin B_{12} coenzymes help recycle folate coenzymes involved in the synthesis of DNA and RNA, and in the normal formation of red blood cells. Vitamin B_{12} prevents degeneration of the myelin sheaths that cover nerves and help maintain normal electrical conductivity through the nerves.

Vitamin-B_{12} deficiency results in *pernicious anemia,* which is caused by a genetic problem in the production of intrinsic factor. When this occurs, folate function is impaired, leading to macrocytic anemia due to interference in normal DNA synthesis. Unlike folate deficiency, the anemia caused by vitamin-B_{12} deficiency is accompanied by symptoms of nerve degeneration, which if left untreated can result in paralysis and death.

Since vitamin B_{12} is well conserved in the body, it is difficult to become deficient from dietary factors alone, unless a person is a strict vegan and consumes a diet devoid of eggs and dairy for several years. Deficiency is usually observed when B_{12} absorption is hampered by disease or surgery to the stomach or ileum, damage to gastric mucosa by alcoholism, or prolonged use of anti-ulcer medications that affect secretion of intrinsic factor. Agerelated decrease in stomach-acid production also reduces absorption of B_{12} in elderly persons. These groups are advised to consume fortified foods or take a supplemental form of vitamin B_{12}.

Choline

For many years, choline was not considered a vitamin because the body makes enough of it to meet its needs in most age groups. However, research now shows that choline production in the body is not enough to cover requirements. Choline is not considered a B vitamin because it does not have a coenzyme function and the amount in the body is much greater than other B vitamins. Choline not only helps maintain the structural integrity of membranes surrounding every cell in the body, but also can play a role in nerve signaling, cholesterol transport, and energy metabolism. An "adequate intake" is 550 milligrams per day for men and 425 milligrams per day for women. Choline is widely found in foods, so it is unlikely that a dietary deficiency will occur.

Vitamin C (Ascorbic Acid)

In 1746, James Lind, a British physician, conducted the first nutrition experiment on human beings in an effort to find a cure for scurvy. However, it was not until nearly 200 years later that ascorbic acid, or vitamin C, was discovered. Vitamin C participates in many reactions by donating electrons as hydrogen atoms. In a reducing reaction, the electron in the hydrogen atom donated by vitamin C combines with other participating molecules, making vitamin

C a reducing agent, essential to the activity of many enzymes. By neutralizing free radicals, vitamin C may reduce the risk of heart disease, certain forms of cancer, and cataracts.

Vitamin C is needed to form and maintain collagen, a fibrous protein that gives strength to connective tissues in skin, cartilage, bones, teeth, and joints. Collagen is also needed for the healing of wounds. When added to meals, vitamin C increases intestinal absorption of iron from plant-based foods. High concentration of vitamin C in white blood cells enables the immune system to function properly by providing protection against oxidative damage from free radicals generated during their action against bacterial, viral, or fungal infections. Vitamin C also recycles oxidized vitamin E for reuse in cells, and it helps folic acid convert to its active form, (THF). Vitamin C helps synthesize carnitine, adrenaline, epinephrine, the neurotransmitter serotonin, the thyroid hormone thyroxine, bile acids, and steroid hormones.

A deficiency of vitamin C causes widespread connective tissue changes throughout the body. Deficiencies may occur in people who eat few fruits and vegetables, follow restrictive diets, or abuse alcohol and drugs. Smokers also have lower vitamin-C status. Supplementation may be prescribed by physicians to speed the healing of bedsores, skin ulcers, fractures, burns, and after surgery. Research has shown that doses up to 1 gram per day may have small effects on duration and severity of the common cold, but not on the prevention of its occurrence.

SOLUBILITY

Solubility is the physical property describing the ability of a given substance, the solute, to dissolve in a solvent. Solubility is measured in terms of the maximum amount of solute dissolved in a solvent at equilibrium. The resulting solution is called a saturated solution. Certain liquids are soluble in all proportions with a given solvent, such as ethanol in water. This property is known as miscibility Under certain conditions the equilibrium solubility can be exceeded to give a so-called supersaturated solution, which is metastable.

In a solution, the solvent is generally a liquid, which can be a pure substance or a mixture. The species that dissolves, the solute, can be a gas, another liquid, or a solid. Solubilities range widely, from infinitely soluble such as ethanol in water, to poorly soluble, such as silver chloride in water. The term insoluble is often applied to poorly soluble compounds, although in some cases insolubility means that a compound is very poorly soluble.

Molecular View

Solubility occurs under dynamic equilibrium, which means that solubility results from the simultaneous and opposing processes of dissolution and precipitation. The solubility equilibrium occurs when the two processes proceed at a constant rate.

The solubility equilibrium is relatively straightforward for "covalent" substances (molecules containing only strong covalent bonds) such as benzene. When dissolved in water, the benzene molecules remain intact but interact with the surrounding molecules of water. When, however, an ionic compound such as sodium chloride (NaCl) dissolves in water, the sodium chloride lattice dissociates into individual ions that are solvated or surrounded by water molecules. Nonetheless, NaCl is said to dissolve in water, because evaporation of the solvent returns crystalline NaCl.

Solubility is also misused to describe the degradation of a compound that accompanies solvolysis. For example, many metals and their oxides are said to be "soluble in hydrochloric acid," whereas the aqueous acid degrades the solid to irreversibly give soluble products. It is also true that most ionic solids are degraded by polar solvents, but such processes are reversible. In those cases where the solute is not recovered upon evaporation of the solvent, the process is referred to as solvolysis. The thermodynamic concept of solubility does not apply straightforwardly to solvolysis.

When a solute dissolves, it may form several species in the solution. For example, an aqueous suspension of ferrous hydroxide, $Fe(OH)_2$, will contain the series

$[Fe(H_2O)_{6-x}(OH)_x]^{(2-x)+}$

as well as other oligomeric species. Furthermore, the solubility of ferrous hydroxide and the composition of its soluble components depends on pH. In general, solubility in the solvent phase can be given only for a specific solute which is thermodynamically stable, and the value of the solubility will include all the species in the solution (in the example above, all the iron-containing complexes).

Factors Affecting Solubility

Solubility is defined for specific phases. For example, the solubility of aragonite and calcite in water are expected to differ, even though they are both polymorphs of calcium carbonate and have the same chemical formula.

The solubility of one substance in another is determined by the balance of intermolecular forces between the solvent and solute, and the entropy change that accompanies the solvation. Factors such as temperature and pressure will alter this balance, thus changing the solubility.

Solubility may also strongly depend on the presence of other species dissolved in the solvent, for example, complex-forming anions (ligands) in liquids. Solubility will also depend on the excess or deficiency of a common ion in the solution, a phenomenon known as the common-ion effect. To a lesser extent, solubility will depend on the ionic strength of solutions. The last two effects can be quantified using the equation for solubility equilibrium.

For a solid that dissolves in a redox reaction, solubility is expected to depend on the potential (within the range of potentials under which the solid remains the thermodynamically stable phase). For example, solubility of gold in high-temperature water is observed to be almost an order of magnitude higher when the redox potential is controlled using a highly-oxidizing Fe_3O_4-Fe_2O_3 redox buffer than with a moderately-oxidizing Ni-NiO buffer.

Solubility (metastable) also depends on the physical size of the crystal or droplet of solute (or, strictly speaking, on the specific or molar surface area of the solute). For quantification, see the equation in the article on solubility equilibrium. For highly defective crystals, solubility may increase with the increasing degree of disorder. Both of these effects occur because of the dependence of solubility constant on the Gibbs energy of the crystal. The last two effects, although often difficult to measure, are of practical importance For example, they provide the driving force for precipitate aging (the crystal size spontaneously increasing with time).

Temperature

The solubility of a given solute in a given solvent typically depends on temperature. For many solids dissolved in liquid water, the solubility increases with temperature up to 100 °C. In liquid water at high temperatures, (e.g., that approaching the critical temperature), the solubility of ionic solutes tends to decrease due to the change of properties and structure of liquid water; the lower dielectric constant results in a less polar solvent.

Gaseous solutes exhibit more complex behavior with temperature. As the temperature is raised, gases usually become less soluble in water, but more soluble in organic solvents.

The chart shows solubility curves for some typical solid inorganic salts Many salts behave like barium nitrate and disodium hydrogen arsenate, and show a large increase in solubility with temperature. Some solutes (e.g. NaCl in water) exhibit solubility which is fairly independent of temperature. A few, such as cerium(III) sulfate, become less soluble in water as temperature increases. This temperature dependence is sometimes referred to as "retrograde" or "inverse" solubility. Occasionally, a more complex pattern is observed, as with sodium sulfate, where the less soluble decahydrate crystal loses water of crystallization at 32 °C to form a more soluble anhydrous phase.

The solubility of organic compounds nearly always increases with temperature. The technique of recrystallization, used for purification of solids, depends on a solute's different solubilities in hot and cold solvent. A few exceptions exist, such as certain cyclodextrins.

Pressure

For condensed phases (solids and liquids), the pressure dependence of solubility is typically weak and usually neglected in practice. Assuming an ideal solution, the dependence can be quantified as

$$\left(\frac{\partial \ln N_i}{\partial P}\right)_T = -\frac{V_{i,aq} - V_{i,cr}}{RT}$$

where the index i iterates the components, N_i is the mole fraction of the ith component in the solution, P is the pressure, the index T refers to constant temperature, $V_{i,\,aq}$ is the partial molar volume of the ith component in the solution, $V_{i,\,cr}$ is the partial molar volume of the ith component in the dissolving solid, and R is the universal gas constant

The pressure dependence of solubility does occasionally have practical significance. For example, precipitation fouling of oil fields and wells by calcium sulfate (which decreases its solubility with decreasing pressure) can result in decreased productivity with time.

Solubility of Gases

Henry's law is used to quantify the solubility of gases in solvents. The solubility of a gas in a solvent is directly proportional to the partial pressure of that gas above the solvent. This relationship is written as:

$$p = kc$$

where k is a temperature-dependent constant (for example, 769.2 L •atm/mol for dioxygen (O_2) in water at 298 K), p is the partial pressure (atm), and c is the concentration of the dissolved gas in the liquid (mol/L).

Polarity

A popular aphorism used for predicting solubility is *"like dissolves like"* This statement indicates that a solute will dissolve best in a solvent that has a similar polarity to itself. This view is rather simplistic, since it ignores many solvent-solute interactions, but it is a useful rule-of-thumb. For example, a very polar (hydrophilic) solute such as urea is very soluble in highly polar water, less soluble in fairly polar methanol, and practically insoluble in non-polar solvents such as benzene. In contrast, a non-polar or lipophilic solute such as naphthalene is insoluble in water, fairly soluble in methanol, and highly soluble in non-polar benzene.

Liquid solubilities also generally follow this rule. Lipophilic plant oils, such as olive oil and palm oil, dissolve in non-polar solvents such as alkanes, but are less soluble in polar liquids such as water.

Synthetic chemists often exploit differences in solubilities to separate and purify compounds from reaction mixtures, using the technique of liquid-liquid extraction.

Rate of Dissolution

Dissolution is not always an instantaneous process. It is fast when salt and sugar dissolve in water but much slower for a tablet of aspirin or a large crystal of hydrated copper(II) sulfate. These observations are the consequence of two factors: the rate of solubilization is related to the solubility product and the surface area of the material. The speed at which a solid dissolves practice, it means that the amount of solute in a solution is not always determined by its thermodynamic solubility, but may depend on kinetics of dissolution (or precipitation).

The rate of dissolution and solubility should not be confused as they are different concepts, kinetic and thermodynamic, respectively.

Quantification of Solubility

Solubility is commonly expressed as a concentration, either by mass (g of solute per kg of solvent, g per dL (100 mL) of solvent), molarity, molality, mole fraction or other similar descriptions of concentration. The maximum equilibrium amount of solute that can dissolve per amount of solvent is the solubility of that solute in that solvent under the specified conditions. The advantage of expressing solubility in this manner is its simplicity, while the disadvantage is that it can strongly depend on the presence of other species in the solvent (for example, the common ion effect).

Solubility constants are used to describe saturated solutions of ionic compounds of relatively low solubility (see solubility equilibrium). The solubility constant is a special case of an equilibrium constant. It describes the balance between dissolved ions from the salt and undissolved salt. The solubility constant is also "applicable" (i.e. useful) to precipitation, the reverse of the dissolving reaction. As with other equilibrium constants, temperature can affect the numerical value of solubility constant. The solubility constant is not as simple as solubility, however the value of this constant is generally independent of the presence of other species in the solvent.

The Flory-Huggins solution theory is a theoretical model describing the solubility of polymers. The Hansen Solubility Parameters and the Hildebrand solubility parameters are empirical methods for the prediction of solubility. It is also possible to predict solubility from other physical constants such as the enthalpy of fusion.

The partition coefficient (Log P) is a measure of differential solubility of a compound in a hydrophobic solvent (octanol) and a hydrophilic solvent (water). The logarithm of these two values enables compounds to be ranked in terms of hydrophilicity (or hydrophobicity).

Applications

Solubility is of fundamental importance in a large number of scientific disciplines and practical applications, ranging from ore processing, to the use of medicines, and the transport of pollutants.

Solubility is often said to be one of the "characteristic properties of a substance," which means that solubility is commonly used to describe the substance, to indicate a substance's polarity, to help to distinguish it from other substances, and as a guide to applications of the substance. For example, indigo is described as "insoluble in water, alcohol, or ether but soluble in chloroform, nitrobenzene, or concentrated sulfuric acid".

Solubility of a substance is useful when separating mixtures. For example, a mixture of salt (sodium chloride) and silica may be separated by dissolving the salt in water, and filtering off the undissolved silica. The synthesis of chemical compounds, by the milligram in a laboratory, or by the ton in industry, both make use of the relative solubilities of the desired product, as well as unreacted starting materials, by-product, and side products to achieve separation.

Another example of this is the synthesis of benzoic acid from phenylmagnesium bromide and dry ice. Benzoic acid is more soluble in an organic solvent such as dichloromethane or diethyl ether, and when shaken with this organic solvent in a separatory funnel, will preferentially dissolve in the organic layer. The other reaction products, including the magnesium bromide, will remain in the aqueous layer, clearly showing that separation based on solubility is achieved. This process, known as liquid-liquid extraction, is an important technique in synthetic chemistry.

Some ionic compounds (salts) dissolve in water, which arises because of the attraction between positive and negative charges (see: solvation). For example, the salt's positive ions (i.e. Ag^+) attract the partially-negative oxygens in H_2O. Likewise, the salt's negative ions (i.e. Cl^-) attract the partially-positive hydrogens in H_2O. Note: oxygen is partially-negative because it is more electronegative than hydrogen, and vice-versa.

$$AgCl_{(s)} \leftrightarrows Ag^+_{(aq)} + Cl^-_{(aq)}$$

However, there is a limit to how much salt can be dissolved in a given volume of water. This amount is given by the solubility product, K_{sp}. This value depends on the type of salt (AgCl vs. NaI, for example), temperature, and the common ion effect.

One can calculate the amount of AgCl that will dissolve in 1 liter of water, some algebra is required.

K_{sp} = $[Ag^+] \times [Cl^-]$ (definition of solubility product)

Ksp = 1.8 × 10-10 (from a table of solubility products)

$[Ag^+]$ = $[Cl^-]$, in the absence of other silver or chloride salts,

$[Ag^+]^2 = 1.8 \times 10^{-10}$

$[Ag^+] = 1.34 \times 10^{-5}$

The result: 1 liter of water can dissolve 1.34×10^{-5} moles of $AgCl_{(s)}$ at room temperature. Compared with other types of salts, AgCl is poorly soluble in water. In contrast, table salt (NaCl) has a higher K_{sp} and is, therefore, more soluble.

Solubility of Organic Compounds

The principle outlined above under polarity, that *like dissolves like,* is the usual guide to solubility with organic systems. For example, petroleum jelly will dissolve in gasoline because both petroleum jelly and gasoline are hydrocarbons. It will not, on the other hand, dissolve in alcohol or water, since the polarity of these solvents is too high. Sugar will not dissolve in gasoline, since sugar is too polar in comparison with gasoline. A mixture of gasoline and sugar can therefore be separated by filtration, or extraction with water.

Solubility in Non-aqueous Solvents

Most publically available solubility values are those for solubility in water. Solubility data for non-aqueous solvents is currently being collected via an open notebook science crowdsourcing project.

Solid Solution

This term is often used in the field of metallurgy to refer to the extent that an alloying element will dissolve into the base metal without forming a separate phase. The solubility line (or curve) is the ine (or lines) on a phase diagram which give the limits of solute addition. That is, the lines show the maximum amount of a component that can be added to another component and still be in solid solution. In microelectronic fabrication, solid solubility refers to the maximum concentration of impurities one can place into the substrate.

Incongruent Dissolution

Many substances dissolve congruently, i.e., the composition of the solid and the dissolved solute stoichiometrically match. However, some substances may dissolve incongruently, whereby the composition of the solute in solution does not match that of the solid. This solubilization is accompanied by alteration of the "primary solid" and possibly formation of a secondary solid phase. However, generally, some primary solid also remains and a complex solubility equilibrium establishes. For example, dissolution of albite may result in formation of gibbsite.

$$NaAlSi_3O_8(s) + H^+ + 7H_2O = Na^+ + Al(OH)_3(s) + 3H_4SiO_4.$$

In this case, the solubility of albite is expected to depend on the solid-to-solvent ratio. This kind of solubility is of great importance in geology, where it results in formation of metamorphic rocks.

13 Viscosity of Water

Viscosity is a measure of the resistance of a fluid which is being deformed by either shear stress or extensional stress. In everyday terms (and for liquids only), viscosity is "thickness". Thus, water is "thin", having a lower viscosity, while vegetable oil is "thick" having a higher viscosity. Viscosity describes a fluid's internal resistance to flow and may be thought of as a measure of fluid friction. For example, high-viscosity magma will create a tall, steep stratovolcano, because it cannot flow far before it cools, while low-viscosity lava will create a wide, shallow-sloped shield volcano. All real fluids (except superfluids) have some resistance to stress, but a fluid which has no resistance to shear stress is known as an "ideal fluid" or "inviscid fluid". The study of viscosity is known as rheology.

Etymology

The word "viscosity" derives from the Latin word "viscum" for mistletoe. A viscous glue was made from mistletoe berries and used for lime-twigs to catch birds.

Viscosity Coefficients

When looking at a value for viscosity, the number that one *m*ost *o*ften sees is the coefficient of viscosity. There are several different viscosity coefficients depending on the nature of applied stress and nature of the fluid. They are introduced in the main books on hydrodynamics and rheology:

- Dynamic viscosity (or absolute viscosity) determines the dynamics of an incompressible Newtonian fluid;
- Kinematic viscosity is the dynamic viscosity divided by the density for a Newtonian fluid;
- Volume viscosity (or bulk viscosity) determines the dynamics of a compressible Newtonian fluid;
- Shear viscosity is the viscosity coefficient when the applied stress is a shear stress (valid for non-Newtonian fluids);
- Extensional viscosity is the viscosity coefficient when the applied stress is an extensional stress (valid for non-Newtonian fluids).

The more usual form of this relationship, called Newton's equation, states that the resulting shear of a fluid is directly proportional to the force applied and inversely proportional to its viscosity. The similarity to Newton's second law of motion (F = ma) should be apparent.

$$\frac{\bar{F}}{A}\eta\frac{\Delta vx}{\Delta z} \text{ or } \frac{F}{A}=\eta\frac{dvx}{dz}$$

$$\Updownarrow \qquad \Updownarrow$$

$$\bar{F}=m\frac{\Delta v}{\Delta t} \text{ or } F=m\frac{dv}{dt}$$

The SI unit of viscosity is the pascal second [Pa·s], which has no special name. Despite its self-proclaimed title as an international system, the International System of Units has had very little international impact on viscosity. The pascal second is rarely used in scientific and technical publications today. The most common unit of viscosity is the dyne second per square centimeter [dyne·s/cm2], which is given the name poise [P] after the French physiologist Jean Louis Poiseuille (1799-1869). Ten poise equal one pascal second [Pa·s] making the centipoise [cP] and millipascal second [mPa·s] identical.

1 pascal second = 10 poise = 1,000 millipascal second

1 centipoise = 1 millipascal second

There are actually two quantities that are called viscosity. The quantity defined above is sometimes called dynamic viscosity, absolute viscosity, or simple viscosity to distinguish it from the other quantity, but is usually just called viscosity. The other quantity called kinematic viscosity (represented by the symbol ? "nu") is the ratio of the viscosity of a fluid to its density.

$$\nu = \frac{\eta}{\rho}$$

Kinematic viscosity is a measure of the resistive flow of a fluid under the influence of gravity. It is frequently measured using a device called a capillary viscometer — basically a graduated can with a narrow tube at the bottom. When two fluids of equal volume are placed in identical capillary viscometers and allowed to flow under the influence of gravity, a viscous fluid takes longer than a less viscous fluid to flow through the tube. Capillary viscometers are discussed in more detail later in this section.

The SI unit of kinematic viscosity is the square meter per second [m^2/s], which has no special name. This unit is so large that it is rarely used. A more common unit of kinematic viscosity is the square centimeter per second [cm^2/

s], which is given the name stokes [St] after the Irish mathematician and physicist George Gabriel Stokes (1819-1903). Even this unit is also a bit too large and so the most common unit is probably the square millimeter per second [mm^2/s] or centistokes [cSt].

1 m^2/s = 10,000 cm^2/s [stokes] = 1,000,000 mm^2/s [centistokes]

1 cm2/s = 1 stokes

1 mm2/s = 1 centistokes

Factors Affecting Viscosity

Viscosity is first and foremost a function of material. The viscosity of water at 20 °C is 1.0020 millipascal seconds (which is conveniently close to one by coincidence alone). Most ordinary liquids have viscosities on the order of 1 to 1000 mPa·s, while gases have viscosities on the order of 1 to 10 μPa·s. Pastes, gels, emulsions, and other complex liquids are harder to summarize. Some fats like butter or margarine are so viscous that they seem more like soft solids than like flowing liquids. Molten glass is extremely viscous and approaches infinite viscosity as it solidifies. Since this process is not as well defined as true freezing, some believe (incorrectly) that glass may still flow even after it has completely cooled, but this is not the case. At ordinary temperatures, glasses are as solid as true solids.

From everyday experience, it should be common knowledge that viscosity varies with temperature. Honey and syrups can be made to flow more readily when heated. Engine oil and hydraulic fluids thicken appreciably on cold days and significantly affect the performance of cars and other machinery during the winter months. In general, the viscosity of a simple liquid decreases with increasing temperature (and vice versa). As temperature increases, the average speed of the molecules in a liquid increases and the amount of time they spend "in contact" with their nearest neighbors decreases. Thus, as temperature increases, the average intermolecular forces decrease. The exact manner in which the two quantities vary is nonlinear and changes abruptly when the liquid changes phase.

Table 13.1: Viscosities of selected materials (note the different unit prefixes)

Simple liquids	T (°C)	η (mPa.s)
Alcohol, ethyl (grain)	20	1.1
Alcohol, isopropyl	20	2.4
Alcohol, methyl (wood)	20	0.59
Blood	37	3-4
Ethylene glycol	25	16.1
Ethylene glycol	100	1.98
Freon 11 (propellant)	-25	0.74
Freon 11 (propellant)	0	0.54
Freon 11 (propellant)	+25	0.42
Freon 12 (refrigerant)	-15	??
Freon 12 (refrigerant)	0	??
Freon 12 (refrigerant)	+15	0.20
Glycerin	20	1420
Glycerin	40	280
Mercury	15	15.5
Milk	25	3
Oil, vegetable, canola	25	57
Oil, vegetable, canola	40	33
Oil, vegetable, corn	20	65
Oil, vegetable, corn	40	31
Oil, vegetable olive	20	84
Oil, vegetable olive	40	??

(Contd...)

Simple liquids	T (°C)	η (mPa.s)
Oil, vegetable, soybean	20	69
Oil, vegetable, soybean	40	26
Oil, machine, light	20	102
Oil, machine, heavy	20	233
Gases	**T (°C)**	**η(μPa.s)**
Air	15	17.9
Hydrogen	0	8.42
Helium	0	18.6
Nitrogen	0	16.7
Oxygen	0	18.1
Complex materials	**T (°C)**	**η (Pa.s)**
Caulk	20	1000
Glass, room temperature		10^{18}-10^{21}
Glass, strain point		$10^{13.6}$
Glass, annealing point		$10^{12.4}$
Glass, softening		$10^{6.6}$
Glass working		10^{3}
Glass, melting		10^{2}
Honey	20	10
Ketchup	20	50
Lard	20	1000
Molasses	20	5
Mustard	25	70
Peanut butter	20	150-250
Sour cream	25	100

(Contd...)

Complex materials	T (°C)	η (Pa.s)
Syrup, chocolate	20	10-25
Syrup, corn	25	2-3
Syrup, maple	20	2-3
Tar	20	30,000
Vegetable shortening	20	1200

Viscosity is normally independent of pressure, but liquids under extreme pressure often experience an increase in viscosity. Since liquids are normally incompressible, an increase in pressure doesn't really bring the molecules significantly closer together. Simple models of molecular interactions won't work to explain this behavior and, to my knowledge, there is no generally accepted more complex model that does. The liquid phase is probably the least well understood of all the phases of matter.

While liquids get runnier as they get hotter, gases get thicker. (If one can imagine a "thick" gas.) The viscosity of gases increases as temperature increases and is approximately proportional to the square root of temperature. This is due to the increase in the frequency of intermolecular collisions at higher temperatures. Since most of the time the molecules in a gas are flying freely through the void, anything that increases the number of times one molecule is in contact with another will decrease the ability of the molecules as a whole to engage in the coordinated movement. The more these molecules collide with one another, the more disorganized their motion becomes. Physical models, advanced beyond the scope of this book, have been around for nearly a century that adequately explain the temperature dependence of viscosity in gases. Newer models do a better job than the older models. They also agree with the observation that the viscosity of gases is roughly independent of pressure and density. The gaseous phase is probably the best understood of all the phases of matter.

Motor Oil

Motor oil is like every other fluid in that its viscosity varies with temperature and pressure. Since the conditions under which most automobiles will be operated can be anticipated, the behavior of motor oil can be specified in advance. In the United States, the organization that sets the standards for performance of motor oils is the Society of Automotive Engineers (SAE). The SAE numbering scheme describes the behavior of motor oils under low and high temperature conditions — conditions that correspond to starting and operating temperatures. The first number, which is always followed by the letter W, describes the low temperature behavior of the oil at start up while the second number describes the high temperature behavior of the oil after the engine has been running for some time. Lower SAE numbers describe oils that are meant to be used under lower temperatures. Oils with low SAE numbers are generally less viscous or runnier than oils with high SAE numbers, which tend to be thicker.

Non-newtonian Fluids

Newton's equation relates shear stress and velocity gradient by means of a quantity called viscosity. A newtonian fluid is one in which the viscosity is just a number. A non-newtonian fluid is one in which the viscosity is a function some mechanical variable like shear stress or time. (Non-newtonian fluids that change over time are said to have a memory.)

Some gels and pastes behave like a fluid when worked or agitated and then settle into a nearly solid state when at rest. Such materials are examples of shear-thinning fluids. House paint is a shear-thinning fluid and it's a good thing, too. Brushing, rolling, or spraying are means of temporarily applying shear stress. This reduces the paint's viscosity to the point where it can now flow out of the applicator and onto the wall or ceiling. Once this shear stress is removed the paint returns to its resting viscosity, which is so large that an appropriately thin layer behaves more like a solid than a liquid and the paint does not run or drip. Think about what it would be like to paint with water or honey for comparison. The former is always too runny and the latter is always too sticky.

Toothpaste is another example of a material whose viscosity decreases under stress. Toothpaste behaves like a solid while it sits at rest inside the tube. It will not flow out spontaneously when the cap is removed, but it will flow out when you put the squeeze on it. Now it ceases to behave like a solid and starts to act like a very thick liquid. When it lands on your toothbrush, the stress is released and the toothpaste returns to a solid (or at least a semisolid) state. You do not have to worry about it flowing off the brush as you raise it to your mouth.

Shear-thinning fluids can be classified into one of three general groups. A material that has a viscosity that decreases under shear stress but stays constant over time is said to be pseudoplastic. A material that has a viscosity that decreases under shear stress and then continues to decrease with time is said to be thixotropic. If the transition from high viscosity (or nearly semisolid) to low viscosity (or essentially liquid) takes place only after the shear stress exceeds some minimum value, the material is said to be a bingham plastic.

Materials that thicken when worked or agitated are called shear-thickening fluids. An example that is often shown in science classrooms is a paste made of cornstarch and water (mixed in the correct proportions). The resulting bizarre good behaves like a liquid when squeezed slowly and an elastic solid when squeezed rapidly. Ambitious science demonstrators have filled tanks with the stuff and then run across it. As long as they move quickly the surface acts like a block of solid rubber, but the second they stop moving the paste behaves like a liquid and the demonstrator winds up taking a cornstarch bath. The shear-thickening behavior makes it a difficult bath to get out of. The harder you work to get out, the harder the material pulls back on you. The only way to escape is to move slowly.

Materials that turn nearly solid under stress are more than just a curiosity. They're ideal candidates for body armor and protective sports padding. A bulletproof vest or a kneepad made of shear-thickening material would be supple and yielding to the mild stresses of ordinary body motions, but would turn rock hard in response to the traumatic stress imposed by a weapon or a fall to the ground.

Shear-thickening fluids are also divided into two groups: those with a time-dependent viscosity (memory materials) and those with a time-independent viscosity (non-memory materials). If the increase in viscosity increases over time, the material is said to be rheopectic. If the increase is roughly directly proportional to the shear stress and does not change over time, the material is said to be dilatant.

Viscosity Measurement

Dynamic viscosity is measured with various types of rheometer. Close temperature control of the fluid is essential to accurate measurements, particularly in materials like lubricants, whose viscosity can double with a change of only 5 °C. For some fluids, it is a constant over a wide range of shear rates. These are Newtonian fluids.

The fluids without a constant viscosity are called Non-Newtonian fluids. Their viscosity cannot be described by a single number. Non-Newtonian fluids exhibit a variety of different correlations between shear stress and shear rate.

One of the most common instruments for measuring kinematic viscosity is the glass capillary viscometer.

In paint industries, viscosity is commonly measured with a Zahn cup, in which the efflux time is determined and given to customers. The efflux time can also be converted to kinematic viscosities (cSt) through the conversion equations. A Ford viscosity cup measures the rate of flow of a liquid. This, under ideal conditions, is proportional to the kinematic viscosity. Also used in paint, a Stormer viscometer uses load-based rotation in order to determine viscosity. The viscosity is reported in Krebs units (KU), which are unique to Stormer viscometers. Vibrating viscometers can also be used to measure viscosity. These models such as the Dynatrol use vibration rather than rotation to measure viscosity. Extensional viscosity can be measured with various rheometers that apply extensional stress. Volume viscosity can be measured with acoustic rheometer.

Liquids

In liquids, the additional forces between molecules become important. This leads to an additional contribution to the shear stress though the exact mechanics of this are still controversial. Thus, in liquids:

- Viscosity is independent of pressure (except at very high pressure); and
- Viscosity tends to fall as temperature increases (for example, water viscosity goes from 1.79 cP to 0.28 cP in the temperature range from 0 °C to 100 °C); see temperature dependence of liquid viscosity for more details.

The dynamic viscosities of liquids are typically several orders of magnitude higher than dynamic viscosities of gases.

Viscosity of Water

The viscosity of water is 8.90×10^{-4} Pa·s or 8.90×10^{-3} dyn·s/cm^2 or 0.890 cP at about 25 °C.

As a function of temperature T (K): μ(Pa·s) = $A \times 10^{B/(T-C)}$

where A=2.414 × 10^{-5} Pa·s ; B = 247.8 K ; and C = 140 K.

14 Alkalinity

Alkalinity

Alkalinity or A_T is a measure of the ability of a solution to neutralize acids to the equivalence point of carbonate or bicarbonate. Alkalinity is closely related to the acid neutralizing capacity (ANC) of a solution and ANC is often incorrectly used to refer to alkalinity. The alkalinity is equal to the stoichiometric sum of the bases in solution. In the natural environment carbonate alkalinity tends to make up most of the total alkalinity due to the common occurrence and dissolution of carbonate rocks and presence of carbon dioxide in the atmosphere. Other common natural components that can contribute to alkalinity include borate, hydroxide, phosphate, silicate, nitrate, dissolved ammonia, the conjugate bases of some organic acids and sulfide. Solutions produced in a laboratory may contain a virtually limitless number of bases that contribute to alkalinity. Alkalinity is usually given in the unit mEq/L (milliequivalent per liter). Commercially, as in the pool industry, alkalinity might also be given in the unit ppm or parts per million.

Alkalinity is sometimes incorrectly used interchangeably with basicity. For example, the pH of a solution can be lowered by the addition of CO_2. This will reduce the basicity; however, the alkalinity will remain unchanged (see example below).

Theoretical Treatment of Alkalinity

In typical groundwater or seawater the measured alkalinity is set equal to:

$$A_T = [HCO_3^-]_T + 2[CO_3^{-2}]_T + [B(OH)_4^-]_T + [OH^-]_T + 2[PO_4^{-3}]T + [HPO_4^{-2}]_T + [SiO(OH)_3^-]_T - [H^+]_{sws} - [HSO_4^-]$$

(Subscript T indicates the total concentration of the species in the solution as measured. This is opposed to the free concentration, which takes into account the significant amount of ion pair interactions that occur in seawater.)

Alkalinity can be measured by titrating a sample with a strong acid until all the buffering capacity of the aforementioned ions above the pH of bicarbonate or carbonate is consumed. This point is functionally set to pH 4.5. At this point, all the bases of interest have been protonated to the zero level species, hence they no longer cause alkalinity. For example, the following reactions take place during the addition of acid to a typical seawater solution:

$$HCO_3^- + H^+ \rightarrow CO_2 + H_2O$$

$$CO_3^{-2} + 2H^+ \rightarrow CO_2 + H_2O$$

$$B(OH)_4^- + H^+ \rightarrow B(OH)_3 + H_2O$$

$$OH^- + H^+ \rightarrow H_2O$$

$$PO_4^{-3} + 2H^+ \rightarrow H_2PO_4^-$$

$$HPO_4^{-2} + H^+ \rightarrow H_2PO_4^-$$

$$[SiO(OH)_3^-] + H^+ \rightarrow [Si(OH)_4^0]$$

It can be seen from the above protonation reactions that most bases consume one proton (H^+) to become a neutral species, thus increasing alkalinity by one per equivalent. CO_3^{-2} however, will consume two protons before becoming a zero level species (CO_2), thus it increases alkalinity by two per mole of CO_3^{-2}. [H^+] and [HSO_4^-] decrease alkalintiy, as they act as sources of protons. They are often represented collectively as $[H^+]_T$.

Alkalinity is typically reported as mg/L as $CaCO_3$. This can be converted into milliequivalent per Liter (mEq/L) by dividing by 50 (the approximate MW of $CaCO_3/2$).

Addition of CO_2

The addition (or removal) of CO_2 to a solution does not change the alkalinity. This is because the net reaction produces the same number of equivalents of positively contributing species (H^+) as negative contributing species (HCO_3^- and/or CO_3^-).

At neutral pH's:

$$CO_2 + H_2O \rightarrow HCO_3^- + H^+$$

At high pH's:

$$CO_2 + H_2O \rightarrow CO_3^{-2} + 2H^+$$

Dissolution of Carbonate Rock

Addition of CO_2 to a solution in contact with a solid can affect the alkalinity, especially for carbonate minerals in contact with groundwater or seawater . The dissolution (or precipitation) of carbonate rock has a strong influence on the alkalinity. This is because carbonate rock is composed of $CaCO_3$ and its dissociation will add Ca^{+2} and CO_3^{-2} into solution. Ca^{+2} will not influence alkalinity, but CO_3^{-2} will increase alkalinity by 2 units.

Alkalinity for Marine Systems

Alkalinity and pH are distinctly different from each other, although their definitions and functions can be easily confused. For those of you as uninformed about water chemistry as I was when I first began, alkalinity is essentially a measurement of water's ability to neutralize acids. It is a measure of the buffering capacity of a system while pH is basically the measurement of the concentration of hydrogen ions in water, in terms of acidity or alkalinity. The alkalinity of water regarding pH issues merely refers to the basic end of a pH scale (alkaline) in contrast to the acidic end of the scale and does not reflect the buffering capacity of a system. It is easy to believe that water with alkaline pH is likely to be high in alkalinity (buffering capacity). However, this is not necessarily true. Water with a high pH, but a low alkalinity is regarded as unstable. Such water will quickly decline in pH with the natural accumulation of organic acids in aquarium systems.

Regarding the care of reef invertebrates, water that is low in alkalinity but high in pH is generally undesirable. Unfortunately, it is not uncommon for aquarists to test their systems and report such conditions. Alkalinity depletion is caused sometimes by the misapplication of calcium supplements and/or a lack of water changes. It occurs naturally, as stated, from the neutralization of acids and removal of carbonates for calcification primarily. Ironically, it is obvious to aquarists that corals need calcium to grow, but carbonates are often ignored. Calcium supplements are some of the first and only products that many aquarists use for reef invertebrates culture. It is often forgotten, however, that coral skeletons are comprised of calcium carbonate. Calcium additions without balanced carbonate additions are about as useless as the keys to one thousand cars in an empty parking lot. And so, misinformed aquarists may continue to dose calcium without noticing any significant growth among corals in the collection (and in observance of an alkalinity that continues to fall). To some extent, an imbalance between free calcium and carbonate levels is natural, although unfriendly at times to successful reef aquariology. Grossly stated, high alkalinity and high calcium levels are mutually exclusive. Simply stated, seawater can only hold so many dissolved solids. As alkalinity increases (the levels of carbonates and bicarbonates) there is less "room" for the saturation of other dissolved elements such as calcium. Calcium and alkalinity in practical applications exist in a tenuous Hi-Lo relationship. Until recently, systems with high alkalinity and low calcium were uncommon because of a poor understanding about alkalinity and the popular application of calcium supplements.

The advent and success of calcium reactors has made some aquarists change their thoughts on ways to maximize calcification. Aquarists are divided on which Hi-Low methodology for maximum calcification works best. Some aquarists dose kalkwasser aggressively to raise calcium levels and accept the coincident drop depression of alkalinity. This technique has grown many corals to impressive size with numerous other benefits from the supplementation of calcium hydroxide. The intent of some aquarists is to maintain calcium levels above 400 ppm.

As such, calcium hydroxide indirectly contributes to the alkalinity of a system by neutralizing acids that would otherwise exhaust buffers from the system. Hydroxide molecules are "spent" rather than carbonate molecules. And so, high calcium and adequate alkalinity can be maintained with the proper application of kalkwasser. While I am inclined to favor this technique for simplicity and the small expense incurred relative to reactor set-ups, it is admittedly difficult to maintain and potentially dangerous when pushed to extreme. It is an error to think that if the addition of x grams of calcium is a good, then 2x grams are better. At calcium levels extending beyond saturation, or during events when calcium is added quickly, it is possible to disturb the balanced relationship between calcium and alkalinity and cause a sudden precipitation of calcium carbonate, commonly known as a "snowstorm", which can have tragic ramifications. Spontaneous precipitation of calcium carbonate occurs when pH levels rapidly climb beyond a certain threshold, which causes crystalline carbonate "snow" to fall out of solution in an essentially insoluble form. The tragedy of the event for a system suffering from this condition is that the reaction must run its course before corrective measures can be taken. The addition of buffers in an attempt to counter the declining alkalinity serves only to feed the precipitous reaction. An aquarist is resigned to watch the spawn of his error to completion, which leaves the buffering capacity of the system at a dangerously low level. The stress of the sudden change in water quality can be significantly harmful to marine organisms as well. Water changes and any methods of damage control that insure stability in the environment will be necessary. Despite the inherent risks, I strongly favor and recommend the use of properly dosed calcium hydroxide in at least small quantities for most systems.

One of the very best ways to maintain alkalinity in reef invertebrates systems is the employment of a calcium reactor. Calcium reactors are vessels filled with calcium carbonate material that is slowly dissolved with a supply of carbon dioxide. Lingering or accumulating carbon dioxide in aquarium systems depletes alkalinity and lowers pH, as the presence of carbon dioxide is neutralized by carbonate ions in seawater. It can also contribute to undesirable growths of algae if neglected. Carbon dioxide and carbonic acid in solution are easily driven off with vigorous aeration. Properly operated, calcium reactors do maintain high alkalinity and reasonably good calcium levels (although they are significantly and proportionately lower). Although they are no less dangerous to use than calcium hydroxide for supplying calcium and alkalinity, calcium reactors are convenient and efficient devices. I strongly recommend the use of calcium reactors for aquarists favoring stony corals in display or culture, and for aquarists displeased with the tedious application of calcium hydroxide. Calcium hydroxide, however, does have additional benefits such as saponification (improving protein skimmer performance) and phosphate precipitation. Many European hobbyists rely on calcium reactors to maintain high levels of alkalinity with supplementation from calcium hydroxide. This has proven to be an excellent methodology for promoting the growth of calcareous organisms.

The oldest and most common method of increasing the buffering capacity of salt water is the addition of sea buffer. Sea buffer is basically (no pun intended) a powdered mix of bicarbonates, carbonates, and borates. Such mixes are designed to increase the alkalinity (buffering capacity) of seawater without raising the pH beyond a set point. Some buffering products do raise the pH of seawater and should only be used with caution. Baking soda, sodium bicarbonate, is a significant portion of most dry mixes of sea buffer. I do not recommend using sodium bicarbonate alone for most aquarists, especially new and less experienced individuals, without the strong admonition that it can raise pH quickly and dangerously without due caution. Baking soda should only be used in small portions when water quality can be tested frequently. Concentrated liquid buffer solutions are becoming popular and seem to be most useful when dosed with proportionate amounts of calcium supplementation in commercial two-part mixes.

It is recommended that alkalinity in captive systems be maintained between 7-12 dKH. There are, in fact, several ways to test for alkalinity in seawater. Some aquarists prefer to measure alkalinity in milliequivalent per liter [meq/L] (the target is more than 3 meq/L). Buffering capacity is also described as carbonate hardness, measured in ppm, but this is only a measure of carbonates and bicarbonate components. Total alkalinity measures all buffers and is higher than carbonate hardness. Commercial test kits for testing alkalinity are sometimes difficult to read. Aquarists who have color blindness, vision impairment or other difficulties in reading colorimetric charts should consult distributors or fellow aquarists (marine aquarium societies, Internet, etc.) on brands of test kits with conspicuous color changes at the titration point.

Lastly, there are implications that difficulties maintaining calcium and alkalinity may be linked to inappropriate magnesium levels. Magnesium should be maintained at roughly three times the level of calcium. High magnesium levels are encountered by inappropriate supplementation and can be lethal to some reef invertebrates. Aquarists have most often reported sensitivity in mollusks and starfish such as "turbo" snails and brittle/serpent starfish. Low magnesium levels, as in economy brand synthetic sea salts have likewise been implicated in difficulties maintaining free calcium and alkalinity adequately. This is yet another reason for maintaining proper water quality through water exchanges and testing with supplementation."

Index

❑❑❑